80 Reasons

No One Should Believe
Dr. Christine Blasey Ford

Other books authored by Michael T. Petro, Jr.

How to Protect Yourself, Home & Family from Violent Criminals (1996; Out-of-Print)

Welcome to Soviet America: Special Edition (2010)

How I Quit Smoking in 31 Days After Smoking for 32 Years! (2012)

Misjudging Separation Of Church And State: 50 Bundled Facts You Won't Learn At Harvard Law School Or Read In The New York Times! (2017)

80 Reasons

No One Should Believe
Dr. Christine Blasey Ford:

Justice Brett Kavanaugh
And The Art Of
Character Assassination!

Michael T. Petro, Jr.

80 Reasons No One Should Believe Dr. Christine Blasey Ford: Justice Brett Kavanaugh & The Art Of Character Assassination!

Author: Michael T. Petro, Jr.

Published by Petro Publications
Cleveland, Ohio USA
PetroPublications.com

Front Cover Photo: Public Domain

Back Cover Photo: Beautiful young woman in cyan tones
ID 157736 © Photoeuphoria | *Dreamstime.com*

ISBN-13: 978-1-7337041-2-0

Dedication

This book is dedicated to the memory of my father and mother. It is further dedicated to all patriotic American citizens of this generation and all previous generations who have risked their lives, limbs, livelihood, and liberty to challenge criminals at all levels, whether foreign or domestic, public or private. I salute those patriotic American culture warriors who are now rising to meet the current threat to truth and freedom within the United States of America!

Thou shalt not bear false witness against thy neighbour

Ninth Commandment
Exodus 20:16
King James Version (KJV)
Holy Bible

After misjudging
"Separation of Church and State,"
in 1980 the Ten Commandments
were erroneously removed from
taxpayer-funded schools by the
U.S. Supreme Court in *Stone v. Graham.*
This may help to explain, in part, why the
Ninth Commandment and others are routinely
violated by leftists in their personal and
professional conduct in the 21st century!

Author Request!

While reviewing *80 Reasons No One Should Believe Dr. Christine Blasey Ford*, keep score of the number of times you believe she committed perjury while testifying under oath to the Senate Judiciary Committee on September 27, 2018.

If you recorded at least one act of perjury, ask yourself this question: Why has Dr. Ford not been charged with perjury? If you recorded multiple acts of perjury, ask yourself why she has not been charged with serial perjury?

Keep in mind the supporters of Dr. Christine Blasey Ford have been working overtime to find just one instance where Justice Brett Kavanaugh (or the man who nominated him – President Trump) made any statement whatsoever that can be interpreted (or misinterpreted) as constituting perjury or some other form of verbal misconduct.

Contents

Chapter Two

Important Introductory Notes

Throughout this book U.S. Supreme Court Associate Justice Brett Kavanaugh is most often referred to as **Judge** Brett Kavanaugh, and occasionally referred to as **Justice** Brett Kavanaugh. This is so because the drama that unfolded as a result of the numerous allegations of sexual misconduct lodged against him occurred while he was a Judge of the U.S. Court of Appeals for the District of Columbia Circuit. Consequently, most of the content herein describes him and his circumstances before he was confirmed by the U.S. Senate and before he was sworn in as an Associate Justice of the U.S. Supreme Court on October 6, 2018.

Also, in order to emphasize various important points, certain words, phrases and sentences have been displayed in bold lettering, as seen in the above paragraph and below. There are numerous quotes in this book, and bold lettering was also added to some of the quoted material. Please note in advance that, except for some headlines, **all bold lettering** was added by this author, and not by the original author of the quoted material.

In addition, the reader will find some material, including some quotes, are repeated throughout this book. Why? Because the repeated quotes and other material were applicable to more than one of the 80 Reasons discussed in Chapter One and also applicable to important points noted in Chapter Two. As you know, repetition is an effective way to drive home a vital point.

When reviewing some of the 80 Reasons the reader may point out that several appear to be "weak;" that is, some could not stand alone as a reason to disbelieve Dr. Christine Blasey Ford. The author agrees, and notes that each individual reason must be evaluated within the context of the other numerous reasons. When each individual reason is viewed within that context, a powerful picture is painted that is impossible to challenge successfully on logical grounds. Also, numerous reasons listed here are absolutely devastating to Dr. Ford's case against Judge Brett Kavanaugh, although only one good reason is needed.

Many examples of fraudulent sexual assault claims are discussed in Chapter Two. Consequently, some readers will criticize this work on the basis that exposing false allegations of sexual misconduct discourages women from coming forward with legitimate complaints. Genuine victims may fear they will be lumped together with fraudsters and subsequently viewed with suspicion by authorities and others. This is particularly true when the accused is a high-profile or powerful individual, such as Bill Clinton, Ted Kennedy, Bill Cosby, or Harvey Weinstein.

This may be true, but the real culprits are the fraudsters and the leftists who aid and abet them. If there were no fraudsters and no leftist support system for them to rely on, there would be no justifiable context within which to doubt genuine victims of sexual misconduct. And yes, there are many indisputable victims across this nation and around the world. However, it is the dishonest accusers who are betraying the sisterhood, not those who expose their dishonestly. Moreover, nothing can justify the deliberate destruction of the character and livelihood of innocent men and boys for personal, political, or professional gain – and every effort must be pursued to discourage this insidious and sinister practice!

Is Dr. Christine Blasey Ford one of those fraudulent accusers? Is she a willing political character assassin? Is she an unwitting pawn of diabolical puppet masters? Or, is she an honest and sincere victim of sexual misconduct? If so, was she correct in identifying a young Brett Kavanaugh as her assailant? After researching an enormous amount of material by her and about her, I have reached my conclusion. You, the reader, are invited to draw your own conclusion after reviewing the 80 Reasons listed in Chapter One and the critical background material contained within Chapter Two.

Chapter One

80 Reasons
No One Should Believe
Dr. Christine Blasey Ford

Dr. Ford's Allegation
Against Judge Brett Kavanaugh

51-year-old Christine Blasey Ford holds a Ph.D. in educational psychology from the University of Southern California. She is currently a professor of psychology at Palo Alto University in Palo Alto, California, and a research psychologist with the Stanford University School of Medicine.

On September 27, 2018, Dr. Christine Blasey Ford testified under oath before the Senate Judiciary Committee. She alleged that when she was 15 years old she had been physically assaulted by 17-year-old Brett Kavanaugh at a small party or gathering. Someone allegedly pushed her into a bedroom and locked the door. In the room the radio volume was increased to preclude her from yelling for help. She was then pushed onto a bed, and Brett Kavanaugh got on top of her. He placed his hand over her mouth, causing her to fear that he may inadvertently kill her. Dr. Ford testified that a young Brett Kavanaugh "groped me and tried to take off my clothes." She further stated that "I believed he was going to rape me."[1]

Allegedly, Mark Judge was also in the room. According to Dr. Ford, Mark Judge jumped onto the bed, toppling the group, allowing her an opportunity to escape into a bathroom across the hall. She claimed both boys were very inebriated and often laughed while the assault occurred.[2]

Judge Brett Kavanaugh's
Opening Response To Dr. Ford's Allegation

53-year-old Brett Kavanaugh is an attorney and a graduate of Yale Law School. Before his elevation to the position of Associate Justice of the Supreme Court of the United States on October 6, 2018, he served for 12 years as a United States Circuit Court Judge of the United States Court of Appeals for the District of Columbia Circuit.

Following Dr. Ford's testimony, on September 27, 2018, Judge Brett Kavanaugh also testified before the Senate Judiciary Committee. He opened with the following statements:

"Less than two weeks ago, Dr. Ford publicly accused me of committing wrongdoing at an event more than 36 years ago when we were both in high school. I denied the allegation immediately, categorically and unequivocally. All four people allegedly at the event, including Dr. Ford's longtime friend, Ms. Keyser, have said they recall no such event. Her longtime friend, Ms. Keyser, said under penalty of felony that she does not know me, and does not believe she ever saw me at a party, ever.

"Here is the quote from Ms. Keyser's attorney's letter: quote, 'Simply put, Ms. Keyser does not know Mr. Kavanaugh, and she has no recollection of ever being at a party or gathering where he was present, with or without Dr. Ford,' end quote. Think about that fact.

"The day after the allegation appeared, I told this committee that I wanted a hearing as soon as possible to clear my name. I demanded a hearing for the very next day. Unfortunately, it took the committee 10 days to get to this hearing. In those 10 long days, as was predictable, and as I predicted, my family and my name have been totally and permanently destroyed by vicious and false additional accusations. The 10-day delay has been harmful to me and my family, to the Supreme Court and to the country."[3]

80 Reasons Dr. Ford's Allegation Is Not Credible

Reason Number One: She doesn't know precisely where the alleged party was held, but initially said it was near a country club.

Dr. Ford was unable to recall precisely **where** the party was held. She said the party wherein she was allegedly assaulted was in a single-family home located near a country club where she had been swimming earlier in the day. But she could not identify a specific house, a specific street, or a specific area; therefore, there is no crime scene to investigate. This convenient lack of recall reflects poorly upon her and weakened her case against Judge Brett Kavanaugh.

Reason Number Two: She could not recall who owned or occupied the house where the alleged party was held.

As Emma Brown of *The Washington Post* wrote, "She [Dr. Ford] also doesn't recall who owned the house or how she got there."[4] Not knowing who owned or occupied the house wherein the alleged party had occurred is a bit unusual given that, for both adolescents and adults, house parties are held at a particular person's house, and the occupant's name is associated with the house and the party. For example, the party, had it occurred, would have been held at "Brett's place," "PJ's place," "Mark's place," or "Leland's house," etc.

For July 1, in his 1982 calendar, 17-year-old Brett Kavanaugh wrote: "Tobin's House – Workout; Go to Timmy's for skis…" He also listed the names of some of the other boys who would also go to "Timmy's."[5] If she did not know who resided in the house at the time of the alleged party, or what name was associated with it, how was she able to know which house to go to?

Reason Number Three: She doesn't know when the alleged party was held!

Dr. Ford was unable to recall precisely **when** the party was held. This makes it impossible for Judge Kavanaugh to produce an alibi for a specific day to clear his name and discredit the allegation against him. This open-ended, variable time frame makes it difficult for investigators to verify or refute her story. Dr. Ford's lack of recall reflects poorly upon her and weakened her allegation against Judge Brett Kavanaugh.

Reason Number Four: She didn't state why the party was held!

Dr. Ford has not stated **why** the party was held. Was it a birthday party? Was it a graduation party? Who invited her? How did she hear about the party? A party that lacks a specific theme, location, and date makes it conveniently difficult for investigators to verify or refute her story. Her lack of important details reflects poorly upon her and weakened her case against Judge Brett Kavanaugh.

Conclusion: Not remembering where, when, or why the party was held, or who occupied the party house, could be justified based upon the fact that the alleged attack occurred 36 years ago. She was allegedly 15 years old at the time, and she would have been traumatized by such an event, if it had, in fact, occurred. However, that holds true only if Dr. Ford's numerous other statements established her as a credible victim and a credible witness. This would provide us with a comfortable context in which we could confidently believe Dr. Ford and find her allegation against Judge Brett Kavanaugh to be credible. But as the reader shall soon discover, regarding numerous other details, Dr. Ford has established herself as an individual who is either chronically deceitful, often confused, delusional, memory impaired, or some combination thereof.

Christine Blasey Ford earned a bachelor's degree in experimental psychology, a master's degree in clinical psychology, a master's degree in epidemiology, and a Ph.D. in educational psychology. She is not a stupid woman! Therefore, we may ask, if she is lying and her story is a fabrication, or, if she is telling the truth and is often confused, delusional, or memory impaired, how can she now function as a competent, trustworthy psychology professor and researcher? How could she function as a credible witness against Judge Brett Kavanaugh or anyone else? How can anyone believe her story?

Reason Number Five: She was unsure how she arrived to the alleged party!

Dr. Ford was unsure how she arrived **to** the party. She claimed in her testimony that someone drove her the night of the party, and they drove her either to the party, from the party, or both. It is possible that she arranged for someone to drive her to the party from the country club where she claims she had been swimming prior to attending the alleged party. But she did not know who drove her!

This lack of recall makes it conveniently difficult for anyone to investigate her story. Also, her lack of recall reflects poorly upon her and weakened her allegation against Judge Brett Kavanaugh.

Reason Number Six: No one has come forward to state that they drove her to the alleged party!

No one has come forward to state that they drove Dr. Ford **to** the party or escorted her **to** the party.

She reportedly lived perhaps seven miles or so from the general location where the party allegedly occurred, and at age 15, she must have been driven to the party by an older person with a driver's license. However, no one has come forward to report that he or she drove Dr. Ford to the party in the 1980s.

Reason Number Seven: She was unsure how she got home from the alleged party!

Dr. Ford was unsure how she returned home **from** the party. Again, she claimed in her testimony that someone drove her the night of the party, and they drove her either to the party, from the party, or both. But she did not know who drove her!

This lack of recall makes it conveniently difficult for anyone to investigate her story. And of course, her repeated lack of recall reflects poorly upon her and weakened her accusation against Judge Brett Kavanaugh.

Reason Number Eight: How did she arrange for a ride home from the alleged party?

Dr. Ford stated that she left the party hurriedly, so she made no phone calls from the house to arrange for a ride home, which was a distance of more than seven miles. No one at the party drove her home, and she had no cell phone in 1982, so how did she arrange for the ride with the unknown driver?

Reason Number Nine: No one has come forward to state that they drove her home from the alleged party!

No one has come forward to state that they drove Dr. Ford home **from** the party or escorted her home **from** the party. Again, Dr. Ford reportedly lived seven miles or so from the general location where the party allegedly occurred, and at age 15, she must have been driven home from the party by an older person with a driver's license. However, no one has come forward to report that he or she drove Dr. Ford home from the party back in the 1980s.

Under oath, Dr. Ford reported that the memory of the assault was seared into her hippocampus, and she was "100 percent" sure that Brett Kavanaugh attacked her. If this is true, why was her recall about numerous events surrounding the alleged assault so dismally poor? Why was she unable to recall where, when and why the party occurred? Why was she unable to recall how she arrived to or from the party?

Conclusion: If Dr. Ford is telling the truth, and she cannot recall how she arrived to the party or how she returned home from the party, it indicates that she has a poor memory. If she is memory impaired, how can Dr. Ford function as a competent, trustworthy psychology professor and researcher? How could she function as a credible witness against Judge Kavanaugh or anyone else? How can anyone believe her story?

If she is lying, then her story is a fabrication and that may explain why she cannot recall how she arrived at the party, how she returned home from the party, why no one has come forward to state that they drove her to the party, and no one has come forward to state that they drove her home from the party. If her story is a fabrication, how can she be trusted to function as a reputable psychology professor and researcher? How could she function as a credible witness against Judge Kavanaugh or any-one else? How can anyone believe her story?

Reason Number Ten: Her reported claustrophobia was contra-dicted by her own behavior!

While under oath, Dr. Ford said she had a second front door added to her Palo Alto, California home because she was claustrophobic due to the alleged physical assault. But the second door was not used as an escape hatch, but as a separate entrance for renters. The second door was an entrance to separate quarters used for marriage counseling services provided by the previous homeowner. Google employees also rented those separate quarters at some point in time. Dr. Ford acknowledged the renting of this space in her home, but by doing so she undermined her contention that the second door was an escape hatch for one who is claustrophobic. She could not escape through a door when she did not have ready access to that door!

Clearly, Dr. Ford's statement that the second door was needed to address her concerns of claustrophobia resulting from an alleged attack by Brett Kavanaugh decades earlier is contradicted by the actual use of the second door.

Which Dr. Ford do you believe, the one who said she installed a second door as an escape hatch because she was claustrophobic, or the Dr. Ford who installed a profit-generating second door to which she did not have ready access?

Reason Number Eleven: Her reported claustrophobia was contradicted by her former boyfriend!

As noted above, Dr. Ford's behavior regarding a second door to her home contradicts her stated need for a second door, allegedly needed to help her deal with claustrophobia. However, in addition to her contradictory behavior, her reported claustrophobia has been refuted by her former boyfriend.

This is the **first** of three refutations by her former boyfriend.

Her former boyfriend, who knew Dr. Christine Blasey Ford for 10 years, dated her from 1992 to 1998 – and who lived with her for several years – said in a sworn statement that she did not report any feelings of claustrophobia during their six year relationship. Nor did he report viewing any symptoms of claustrophobia in Dr.

Ford. According to her former boyfriend, in California "she ended up living in a very small, 500 sq. ft. house with one door."[6]

Who do you believe, Dr. Ford or her former boyfriend?

Reason Number Twelve: Her fear of flying was contradicted by her behavior!

While under oath, Dr. Ford expressed a fear of flying, thus causing hesitation in her decision to participate in the U.S. Senate Judiciary Committee hearing regarding her allegation against Judge Kavanaugh. This delayed the hearing by about one week.

The report by Rachel Mitchell, the highly experienced sex crimes prosecutor who questioned Dr. Ford on behalf of Senate Judiciary Committee Republicans, stated that, during her testimony Dr. Ford acknowledged that she flies fairly frequently for hobbies and for work; she flies once each year to visit her family; she had flown to Hawaii, French Polynesia, as well as Costa Rica. In addition, Dr. Ford flew to Washington, D.C. to testify before the Senate Judiciary Committee.[7]

On *Life, Liberty & Levin*, Mollie Hemmingway, The Federalist Senior Editor and *Fox News* Contributor, described Dr. Ford as a "global frequent flyer," while Dr. Ford claimed she feared flying to attend the Senate Judiciary Committee hearings.[8]

Which Dr. Ford do you believe, the one who says she has a fear of flying, or the one who frequently flies?

Reason Number Thirteen: Her fear of flying was contradicted by her former boyfriend!

In a sworn statement, her former boyfriend reported that Dr. Ford neither reported nor exhibited a fear of flying during their six-year relationship. He said they even flew together in a propeller-driven plane when they vacationed in Hawaii. Dr. Ford acknowledged that she flew when she took vacations.

This is the **second** of three refutations by her former boyfriend.

According to her former boyfriend, "While visiting Ford in Hawaii, we traveled around the Hawaiian islands including one time on a propeller plane. Dr. Ford never indicated a fear of flying. To the best of my recollection, Dr. Ford never expressed a fear of closed quarters, tight spaces, or places with only one exit."[9]

By portraying herself as a victim who fears enclosed spaces and flying, in the minds of U.S. Senators and millions of television viewers, Dr. Ford painted a picture of herself as a fragile "Damsel in Distress" in need of sympathy and protection. Before agreeing to attend the Senate hearings, her lawyers said Dr. Ford would attend the hearings only if they were structured in a way that was "fair" and would "ensure her safety." Was this psychologist (or her handlers) using psychology to manipulate the minds of U.S. Senators and TV viewers?

Reason Number Fourteen: Her lack of knowledge of polygraphs was contradicted!

Dr. Ford and her attorneys reported that she passed a polygraph test regarding her allegation against Judge Kavanaugh. Initially, her attorneys refused to turn over the test results to the U.S. Senate. More importantly, while under oath, Dr. Ford reported that she had never spoke to anyone regarding "how to take a polygraph." However, her former boyfriend said Dr. Ford had coached a friend (who later became an FBI agent) and explained "in detail what to expect" when taking a polygraph test.[10]

This is the **third** of three refutations by her former boyfriend.

Again, was this psychologist using psychology to help a friend deceive those who questioned her via a polygraph test? Did this psychologist use her knowledge of psychology to help her pass the polygraph test that was recently administered to her regarding her allegation against Judge Kavanaugh?

Concluding Questions: Who do you believe, Dr. Ford or her former boyfriend who has contradicted her statements regarding (1) her alleged claustrophobia and need for a second door to her home, (2) her alleged fear of flying, (3) and her alleged lack of knowledge regarding polygraph testing?

If she is telling the truth, then her former boyfriend repeatedly lied in a sworn statement to the Senate Judiciary Committee. If she is not telling the truth, is confused, delusional, or is memory impaired, how can Dr. Ford function as a competent, trustworthy psychology professor and researcher? How could she function as a credible witness against Judge Kavanaugh or anyone else? How can anyone believe her story?

Reason Number Fifteen: She scratched out the word "early" from her handwritten polygraph test statement!

Dr. Ford produced a one-page, handwritten statement describing the alleged attack by Judge Brett Kavanaugh. Once hooked up to the polygraph testing device, she would be asked only two questions regarding her handwritten statement:

13

Question Number One: "Is any part of your statement false?"

Dr. Ford's answer: "No!"

Question Number Two: "Did you make up any part of your statement?"

Dr. Ford's answer: "No!"

The polygraph examiner, Jeremiah Hanafin, determined that her two answers were "not indicative of deception."[11]

However, Guy Benson of *Townhall.com* noted that, in her handwritten statement Dr. Ford, "...originally wrote that the attack had taken place in the 'early 80's,' then scratched out the word 'early' before the test was administered."[12]

Why would Dr. Ford scratch out the word "early" on her statement used for the polygraph test when she claimed that the assault took place in the "early" 1980s?

It therefore appears Dr. Ford manipulated her polygraph test so she would not be required to answer a question regarding approximately when in the 1980s the alleged assault took place. This is very suspicious behavior!

Reason Number Sixteen: Her handwritten polygraph test statement appears to be a "word salad."

At first glance, the handwritten statement Dr. Ford prepared to serve as the basis for her polygraph questioning has the appearance of what psychologists and psychiatrists refer to as a "word salad." According to *Merriam-Webster.com*, a word salad is defined as "extremely disorganized speech or writing." It is a symptom of a mental disorder, and is often associated with schizophrenia.

The one-page handwritten statement prepared by Dr. Ford is available at *USAtoday.com*,[13] along with other details describing the polygraph testing procedure. If you visit that site you will find a letter with the heading: Katz, Marshall & Banks. Scroll down to view the statement prepared by Dr. Ford for her polygraph exam. By anyone's standards, it may accurately be referred to as "chicken scratch." I counted at least a dozen words, letters, etc. that had been scratched out. Although it is very short, it is laborious to read. It looks more like a statement prepared by an insecure, indecisive, uneducated child, not a Ph.D. level psychologist and researcher.

When questioned by Rachel Mitchell as to whether or not someone helped her prepare her handwritten statement for the polygraph test, Dr. Ford said, "No, but you can tell how anxious I was by the terrible handwriting."

Several questions immediately surface: Firstly, does this "word salad" facilitate deception when used as the basis for polygraph questioning? It certainly does appear that the author was having enormous difficulty in presenting a clear, straightforward summary of a very important event. Was that intentional? Confusing statements will produce confusing responses during polygraph questioning! In addition, if Dr. Ford was telling the truth, why was she so nervous?

Reason Number Seventeen: She claimed she did not know if her polygraph session had been recorded via video or audio!

Margot Cleveland, an adjunct professor for the college of business at the University of Notre Dame, stated the following: "And when discussing the polygraph, Ford again feigns ignorance and begins to lie re whether it was video or audio taped and then realizes she better admit the truth."[14]

After reviewing the transcript of Dr. Ford's testimony regarding polygraph testing, my conclusion was not as harsh as the one reached by Margot Cleveland. In her initial response it appears Dr. Ford may have been either evasive or perhaps ignorant when asked if she knew whether or not the polygraph session was recorded. She eventually admitted that she assumed the session was audiotaped and videotaped because a computer had been set up by the polygraph examiner. But she said she still did not know for sure if the session was recorded.

This testing behavior reflects poorly on her credibility! As an experienced medical researcher she would have been involved in many testing and experimental procedures that require special attention to every detail. As a psychology professor she would be familiar with hundreds – or perhaps even thousands – of experiments found in textbooks and relevant psychological and medical journals – all of which demand special attention to every detail. So why was she so inattentive during her polygraph testing procedure – as she claimed?

When asked by sex crimes expert Rachel Mitchell if she knew who paid for the polygraph test, she again claimed ignorance. However, because her Democrat political activist lawyers offered to help her prevent Judge Kavanaugh from being elevated to the U.S. Supreme Court at no cost to her, she may have assumed they would pay for the procedure – and she should have stated so! (A transcript of Dr. Ford's complete testimony is available at *WashingtonPost.com*.)[15]

Reason Number Eighteen: She claimed she could not recall if her polygraph session had occurred the day of her grandmother's funeral or the day after.

Again, this is strange behavior from a trained observer, especially in light of the fact that the polygraph test was taken just one month earlier. It appears at this point that Dr. Ford may have been trying to manipulate the viewing audience and establish herself as a frightened "Damsel in Distress" who is in need of sympathy. This would help explain why her attorneys wanted Dr. Ford to be questioned exclusively by the white male Republican senators and not by a highly skilled, soft-spoken, sympathetic, female interrogator such as Rachel Mitchell.

In addition, by not having answers to secondary and tertiary questions, her failure to answer primary questions such as where, when, and why the party was held, are less likely to stand out and make it appear as if she fails to recall only critically important details. Yes, it appears manipulative psychology was at work here! Again, this behavior reflects poorly on her credibility!

Reason Number Nineteen: It was inappropriate to conduct a polygraph exam while Dr. Ford was grieving the loss of her grandmother.

In her report, sex crimes prosecutor Rachel Mitchell correctly stated that "It would also have been inappropriate to administer a polygraph to someone who was grieving." This should have been obvious to Dr. Christine Blasey Ford, a psychologist, to her attorneys, and to the polygraph examiner. Grieving the loss of her grandmother most certainly had the potential to influence Dr. Ford's physiological responses to the polygraph test questions in unpredictable ways! (The complete report issued by Rachel Mitchell is available at *Breitbart.com*.)[16]

Reason Number Twenty: Her polygraph test results are not consistent with her stated level of anxiety during the testing procedure!

Recall the following from Reason Number Sixteen: When questioned by Rachel Mitchell as to whether or not someone helped her prepare her handwritten statement for the polygraph test, Dr. Ford said, "No, but you can tell how anxious I was by the terrible handwriting."

So, if Dr. Ford was extremely anxious during the polygraph testing procedure, as she had claimed, why was her high level of anxiety not reflected in the test results? If she was very nervous during the exam, the polygraph machine should have indicated that she was, in fact, very nervous, and thus would have suggested that she was not telling the truth! As noted under Reason Number Fifteen, the polygraph examiner determined that her two answers were "not indicative of deception," thus she exhibited no physiological symptoms of anxiety when tested. The only sign of anxiety was found in her mysteriously and conveniently generalized and seemingly incoherent handwritten statement upon which the polygraph test was based.

Was Dr. Ford anxious on the outside, but not on the inside?

This is very suspicious in light of the following statement by Bart Marcois of *opslens.com*: "Polygraph tests are manna from Heaven for subjects with certain psychological disorders. They have nearly no effect on sociopaths, psychopaths, or people with borderline personality disorder. Anyone who is not overly burdened with a conscience or empathy has no trouble lying, and therefore no trouble passing a lie detector. But they also are easy to pass when the test subject feels no connection with or respect for the test administrator."[17]

As a psychologist – and one who allegedly coached a friend on how to pass a polygraph test – Dr. Ford most certainly should be aware of the psychological conditions that influence polygraph test results. Therefore, she should be very knowledgeable of how to deceive the machine and her examiner.

Based on what Dr. Ford and her attorneys most probably know about the reliability of polygraph test results, we may conclude that the polygraph test was taken by Dr. Ford for political reasons, not legal reasons. Only in the court of public opinion would polygraph test results carry a lot of weight!

If Dr. Ford had "flunked" the polygraph test, would we have ever learned about those results? Did she take – and flunk – polygraph tests before the one taken and passed on August 7, 2018? We may never know!

Reason Number Twenty-One: The name "Kavanaugh" was not a part of the polygraph testing statement or procedure!

As previously noted, in her one-page handwritten statement used as the basis for the polygraph test, Dr. Ford laid out her basic allegation against Judge Brett Kavanaugh. However, in addition to scratching out the word "early," she also left out the name "Kavanaugh." Instead, she simply stated that she had been attacked by "Brett," but not Brett Kavanaugh! She also wrote in the name Mark, but did not name Mark Judge.

As noted by Jonathan Turley, a law professor at George Washington University Law School, "The most notable aspect of the story however is the only two 'relevant' questions asked by Hanafin 'Is any part of your statement false?' and 'Did you make up any part of your statement?'"

Professor Turley added, "Those questions would be effectively useless in an actual case. Good polygraphers ask specific, clear, insular questions. They do not use overarching language. He did not ask specific questions on whether she was assaulted by Kavanaugh – a rather curious omission."[18]

Reason Number Twenty-Two: The name "Judge" was not a part of the polygraph testing statement or procedure!

As previously noted, in her one-page handwritten statement used as the basis for the polygraph test, Dr. Ford laid out her basic allegation against Judge Brett Kavanaugh. However, in addition to scratching out the word "early" and leaving out the name "Kavanaugh," she simply wrote in the name "Mark," but did not specifically name Mark Judge.

All this lack of specificity provides for a lot of "wiggle room" wherein one can refrain from telling the truth without detection. To determine whether or not Dr. Ford was telling the truth about her allegation against Judge Kavanaugh, direct, specific questions should have been asked that included the full names of Brett Kavanaugh and Mark Judge.

Perhaps most importantly, as noted elsewhere in this book, Dr. Ford earned a master's degree in epidemiology from the Stanford University School of Medicine. She focused on biostatistics. Dr. Ford also worked as the director of biostatistics at Corcept Therapeutics, and she collaborated with FDA statisticians. In addition, Dr. Ford has expertise in designing statistical models for research projects. As professional researchers know, a faulty design will lead to faulty conclusions. She is also a published author.

So, Dr. Ford works in the complex field of biostatistics and she designs statistical research models to ensure the accuracy of outcomes. To be successful in these areas requires enormous attention to detail; it demands great specificity. To become a published author also requires great attention to detail. So, in an important document, such as her handwritten statement regarding the alleged attack by Brett Kavanaugh, why did she avoid specificity? Why was it lacking in important details such as the last names of the two boys she accused of assault? Why did her handwritten statement lack the critical detail of the word "early?"

As a psychologist, as a professor, as a researcher, as a published author, why would she design for her polygraph test a vaguely written statement regarding her allegation against Judge Brett Kavanaugh? Was it designed to ensure a faulty outcome, that is, to ensure a false negative that made her appear truthful when she was not?

Reason Number Twenty-Three: The American Psychological Association (APA) has determined that polygraph test results are unreliable!

According to the American Psychological Association, "The accuracy (i.e., validity) of polygraph testing has long been controversial. An underlying problem is theoretical: There is no evidence that any pattern of physiological reactions is unique to deception." In addition, "An honest person may be nervous when answering truthfully and a dishonest person may be non-anxious. Also, there are few good studies that validate the ability of polygraph procedures to detect deception."[19]

Reason Number Twenty-Four: The U.S. Supreme Court has ruled that polygraph test results are unreliable!

The U.S. Supreme Court has ruled that polygraph testing produces unreliable results, therefore, polygraph test results carry no weight in a court of law.

In the 1998 case of *U.S. v. Scheffer*, the U.S. Supreme Court ruled that, "[T]here is simply no consensus that polygraph evidence is reliable. To this day, the scientific community remains extremely polarized about the reliability of polygraph techniques."[20]

Dr. Ford's attorneys most certainly know that, based on this U.S. Supreme Court conclusion, polygraph test results carry no weight in a court of law in the United States. Therefore, they should carry no weight in Senate Judiciary Committee hearings, especially in this case – in light of the numerous shenanigans associated with Dr. Ford's polygraph exam – and her dubious behavior throughout this ordeal.

Reason Number Twenty-Five: Dr. Ford conducted graduate level studies on self-hypnosis and meditation that could influence polygraph test results.

According to former Clinton advisor Dick Morris,[21] Dr. Ford conducted graduate level studies on self-hypnosis, meditation, and how to pass a polygraph test by controlling one's responses to examiner questions. If this is true, that would explain why this psychologist subjected herself to such testing, which is quite unusual given that polygraph test results are not admissible in a court of law – but carry a lot of weight in the court of public opinion!

Reason Number Twenty-Six: She was accused of credit card fraud!

In addition to contradicting Dr. Ford's claim that she suffered from claustrophobia, feared flying, and had no previous knowledge of polygraph testing, her former boyfriend also accused Dr. Ford of credit card fraud. Allegedly, about a year after they separated Dr. Ford charged $600.00 on one of his credit cards – then lied about it. She admitted committing credit card fraud only after her former boyfriend threatened to contact fraud investigators. In his letter the former boyfriend also indicated that he severed their romantic relationship when he discovered she had been "unfaithful." (The letter submitted by Dr. Ford's former boyfriend is available at *rwnofficial.com*.)[22]

Concluding Question: If her former boyfriend is telling the truth in his sworn statement regarding Dr. Christine Blasey Ford engaging in credit card fraud and lying about it, how could anyone trust her to be a credible witness against Judge Brett Kavanaugh or anyone else? How can anyone believe her story?

Reason Number Twenty-Seven: Mark Judge refuted the core allegation within her story!

Under oath, Dr. Ford stated that Mark Judge, a high school friend of Brett Kavanaugh, was in the room where the alleged assault took place and witnessed the event. However, in a letter to Judiciary Chairman Chuck Grassley, Mark Judge wrote, "In fact, I have no memory of this alleged incident." He also stated that, "Brett Kavanaugh and I were friends in high school but I do not recall the party described in Dr. Ford's letter. More to the point, I never saw Brett act in the manner Dr. Ford describes."[23]

Mark Judge is the **first** of four credible people to refute Dr. Ford's statement regarding the alleged party and alleged attack.

Reason Number Twenty-Eight: Why was she friendly towards Mark Judge shortly after he allegedly participated in an attack against her that reportedly left her traumatized?

According to Daniel Payne of *USAtoday.com*, Dr. Ford reported that about six to eight weeks after the alleged attack, she met Mark Judge at a Safeway supermarket where he was employed at the time. She reportedly said "Hello" to Mark Judge, but he was "very uncomfortable saying 'Hello' back."

Daniel Payne thus asked the following question: "Why did Ford talk to Mark Judge after he allegedly participated in an assault on her?" Dr. Ford said she was so traumatized by the alleged attack that she became claustrophobic and had to install an additional door to her home. In addition, she reported "anxiety, phobia and PTSD-like symptoms." More than three decades later she still had difficulty dealing with the impact of that event. Because of that lingering emotional damage "Ford's attorneys demanded that she not even appear in the same room as Kavanaugh at the same time; and this is over 30 years after the alleged assault, not 'six to eight weeks.'"

Daniel Payne concluded that, "This is rather astonishing!"[24]

Reason Number Twenty-Nine: Patrick J. Smyth refuted a critical part of her story!

Dr. Ford stated that Patrick J. Smyth was present at the party when the alleged assault took place. However, Patrick J. Smyth has refuted Dr. Ford's claim. Smyth's attorney, Eric Bruce, released the following statement: "He [Patrick J. Smyth] truthfully answered every question the FBI asked him and, consistent with the information he previously provided to the Senate Judiciary Committee, he indicated that he has no knowledge of the small party or gathering described by Dr. Christine Blasey Ford nor does he have any knowledge of the allegations of improper conduct she has leveled against Brett Kavanaugh."[25]

Patrick J. Smyth is the **second** of four credible people to refute Dr. Ford's statement regarding the alleged party and the alleged attack.

Reason Number Thirty: Within a short period of time she contradicted herself regarding her description of the role of Patrick J. Smyth.

Dr. Ford described Patrick J. Smyth as a "bystander" to her polygrapher and in a July 6, 2018 text to *The Washington Post*. However, in her testimony to the Senate Judiciary Committee she said it would be inaccurate to describe him as a "bystander."[26] Which Dr. Christine Blasey Ford do you believe, the one who described Patrick J. Smyth as a bystander, or the one who said it would be inaccurate to describe him as a bystander?

Reason Number Thirty-One: Leland Ingham Keyser refuted a crucial part of her story.

Dr. Ford stated that her lifelong friend, Leland Ingham Keyser, was present at the party when the alleged assault took place. However, Leland Ingham Keyser refuted Dr. Ford's claim. Guy Benson of *Townhall.com* wrote, "This final named witness is a female, a Democrat, and a longtime friend of the accuser. She states outright not only that she doesn't recall attending this particular alleged party, but that she never knew Kavanaugh and was never at any party with him, as far as she can recall."[27]

To her credit, Leland Ingham Keyser did not retract or alter her statement when pressured by Dr. Ford supporters to "clarify" her statement.[28]

Leland Ingham Keyser is the **third** of four credible people to refute Dr. Ford's statement regarding the alleged party and the alleged attack.

Reason Number Thirty-Two: She did not warn her friends!

According to Dr. Ford, before she left the party, or as she left the party, she did not warn her female friend that she, too, may be at risk. In addition, she did not warn Leland Ingram Keyser or any other girls that they could be at risk if they attended future parties with these boys.

If Dr. Ford is telling the truth, it indicates she displayed a callous disregard for the safety of her female friends. If she is lying, there would be no need to warn them, and that would explain why no warning was issued.

Reason Number Thirty-Three: Judge Brett Kavanaugh refuted the core allegation within her story.

Under oath, Dr. Ford stated that Brett Kavanaugh physically assaulted her at a summer party when they were both teenagers in high school. However, Judge Brett Kavanaugh refuted Dr. Ford's claim that he assaulted her 36 years earlier. Under oath, Judge Brett Kavanaugh stated that he never assaulted Dr. Ford or anyone else.

Judge Brett Kavanaugh is the **fourth** of four credible people to refute Dr. Ford's statement regarding the alleged party and the alleged attack.

Guy Benson of *Townhall.com* concluded that, "So of the five people Ford places at this party 36 years ago, she is the only one who says it even took place. The other four have contradicted or rejected her memory of it, to varying degrees. This means that in addition to having zero contemporaneous corroboration of the assault happening (Ford says she told nobody for 30 years), we do not even have any current corroboration that the alleged party occurred at all, based on the testimony of all other individuals Ford herself has named as the only other attendees."[29]

Concluding Questions: Who do you believe, Dr. Ford or (1) Mark Judge, (2) Patrick J. Smyth, (3) Leland Ingham Keyser, and (4) Judge Brett Kavanaugh – all four of whom have contradicted her statement regarding the alleged party and the alleged physical assault? Judge Brett Kavanaugh, under American jurisprudence, has the presumption of innocence to support his denial.

Dr. Ford has no evidence and no witnesses to support her allegation. All of her so-called witnesses have stated they did not witness what Dr. Ford has alleged. If she is telling the truth, then Mark Judge, Patrick J. Smyth, Leland Ingham Keyser, and Judge Brett Kavanaugh are either lying, confused, delusional, or have poor memories.

If she is not telling the truth, is confused, delusional, or is memory impaired, how can Dr. Ford function as a competent, trustworthy psychology professor and researcher? How could she function as a credible witness against Judge Kavanaugh or anyone else? How can anyone believe her story?

Reason Number Thirty-Four: Judge Brett Kavanaugh's 1982 calendar supported his claim of innocence!

While Dr. Ford had changed the general time period wherein the alleged attacked supposedly occurred, she settled on the summer of 1982. However, as noted elsewhere, like his father, young Brett Kavanaugh kept a calendar during that time period which documented his whereabouts and activities. Nowhere on his calendar did he record a party or gathering in the general location where the party supposedly occurred or during the time period alleged by Dr. Ford.

While this is not solid proof of Judge Brett Kavanaugh's innocence, it does substantiate his claim of innocence and it is just one more reason to disbelieve Dr. Christine Blasey Ford. Each of her individual statements must be gauged within the context of all her other statements and the statements of the many individuals who have contradicted her.

Democrat Senator Sheldon Whitehouse noted that Judge Brett Kavanaugh's calendar showed he attended a party on July 1, 1982, and this may be the "smoking gun" to demonstrate he is guilty as charged and further committed perjury. However, as noted by Guy Benson of *Townhall.com*, Dr. Ford said the party she attended took place close to the country club where she had been swimming. But the party noted in Judge Kavanaugh's calendar occurred at a location 11 miles from the country club.

Dr. Ford said the party she attended was in a single-family home, but the structure wherein the July 1st party occurred was a townhouse. In addition, one of the boys who attended the July 1st party had dated Dr. Ford for several months, but Dr. Ford did not list him as one of the boys at the party wherein she claims she was assaulted by a young, drunken, Brett Kavanaugh. She certainly would have remembered him as an attendee at the party she allegedly attended, but did not list him as such. So, there was no smoking gun – only wishful thinking![30]

Reason Number Thirty-Five: She changed the number of attackers!

Dr. Ford stated in 2018 that two boys were involved in the alleged assault, specifically Brett Kavanaugh and Mark Judge. However, in the notes taken by her therapist in 2012 it was recorded that Dr. Ford said there were four boys who were involved in the alleged assault. Dr. Ford explained this as an error by the therapist, noting that there were four boys at the party but only two boys in the room when she was attacked.[31]

Reason Number Thirty-Six: She changed her stated age!

Dr. Ford changed her story regarding her age when the alleged assault took place. In 2018 she said she was 15 years old, or in her "early teens," when the alleged assault took place. Her therapist's 2012-13 notes, however, indicate that Dr. Ford's stated she was in her "late teens" when the alleged assault took place.[32]

Reason Number Thirty-Seven: She changed the time period!

Dr. Ford changed her story regarding the time period wherein the alleged assault took place. She stated in 2018 that the alleged assault took place in 1982, or in the "early 80s." Her therapist's 2012 notes indicate that Dr. Ford stated the alleged assault took place in the "mid 80s."

Concluding Questions: Which Dr. Ford do you believe, the Dr. Ford who told her therapist in 2012 that four boys were involved in the alleged assault, or the Dr. Ford who told the Senate Judiciary Committee in 2018 that two boys were involved in the alleged assault?

Which Dr. Ford do you believe, the Dr. Ford who told her therapist in 2012 that the alleged assault occurred when she was in her "late teens," or the Dr. Ford who told the Senate Judiciary Committee in 2018 that the alleged assault occurred when she was in her "early teens?"

Which Dr. Ford do you believe, the Dr. Ford who told her therapist in 2012 that the alleged assault occurred in the "mid 80s," or the Dr. Ford who told the Senate Judiciary Committee in 2018 that the alleged assault occurred in the "early 80s?"

Reason Number Thirty-Eight: She was wrong about identifying Kavanaugh during therapy!

Dr. Ford said the notes taken by her therapist in 2012 would support her 2018 allegation against Judge Kavanaugh. However, in the notes taken by her therapist in 2012 Brett Kavanaugh's name was not recorded as the individual who allegedly assault-ed her.[33]

Reason Number Thirty-Nine: She withheld her therapy notes from the Senate Judiciary Committee, but shared them with *The Washington Post*.

As noted by Phillip Klein of the *WashingtonExaminer.com*, "The [therapy] notes, which are touted as the single piece of docu-mentary evidence of her previously describing the assault, were not turned over to the committee."[34]

According to *FoxNews.com*, "Grassley also demanded Ford's attorneys hand over notes from her 2012 therapy sessions in which she claimed to have discussed her alleged sexual assault decades ago. The senator said it was 'not justified' any longer for Ford to cite privacy and medical privilege given that she has relied on them extensively as a kind of corroborating evidence to implicate Kavanaugh."[35]

Why did she withhold such important documentation from the Senate Judiciary Committee? What did she not want them to see?

Reason Number Forty: Dr. Ford and her attorneys also withheld her polygraph testing information from the Senate Judiciary Committee.

On October 3, 2018, John Nolte of *Breitbart.com* wrote, "As of this writing, Ford's legal team is still refusing to release either her polygraph information or therapist notes to the Senate Judiciary Committee."[36]

Reason Number Forty-One: Dr. Ford and her attorneys also withheld from the Senate Judiciary Committee her communications with the media.

As reported by *FoxNews.com*, "Additionally, Grassley requested copies of communications between Ford and the media describing her allegations, saying that the legal team's failure to provide Ford's full correspondence with *The Washington Post* suggested a 'lack of candor.'"

In frustration, Senator Chuck Grassley, the Chairman of the Senate Judicial Committee, said, "Your continued withholding of material evidence despite multiple requests is unacceptable as the Senate exercises its constitutional responsibility of advice and consent for a judicial nomination."

According to *FoxNews.com*, "Senate Judiciary Committee Chairman Chuck Grassley demanded that attorneys for Ford turn over her therapist notes and other key materials, and suggested she was intentionally less than truthful about her experience with polygraph examinations during Thursday's dramatic Senate hearing."[37]

Reason Number Forty-Two: She changed the number of party attendees.

Dr. Ford changed her story regarding the number of people who attended the alleged party. In her letter to Senator Feinstein, Dr. Ford stated that five people attended the party, her and four others (three boys and two girls). But in her sworn testimony to the Senate Judiciary Committee she said there were six people at the party, her and five others (four boys and two girls).

She changed her story from three boys, all of whom she had named, to four boys. Why did she do this? She had to

31

conveniently add an unknown fourth boy because none of the three boys she mentioned lived near the country club where she originally said the party took place. So, she had to add a fourth unknown boy, and we would assume he lived near the country club, and that would be presumed to be the house wherein the party took place. Because the fourth boy is unknown, there is no party house to investigate to refute her story. A very convenient change, indeed![38]

Which Dr. Ford do you believe, the Dr. Ford who said five people attended the party, or the Dr. Ford who said six people attended the party?

Reason Number Forty-Three: An unnamed fourth boy has not come forward.

As stated above, Dr. Ford changed her story and said that in addition to Brett Kavanaugh, Mark Judge, and Patrick J. Smyth, there was a fourth boy who attended the party. However, no one has come forward to state that he was the fourth boy at the party.[39]

Reason Number Forty-Four: She changed the general location of the party.

When sex crimes expert Rachel Mitchell showed maps to Dr. Ford during her Senate Judiciary Committee hearing, she changed the location of the alleged party from "near" the country club to somewhere between the country club and her home. As Margot Cleveland has noted, Dr. Ford made this change when it became apparent that none of the boys she mentioned as party attendees lived near the country club; therefore, the party was not likely to have taken place near the country club as she had claimed.[40]

Reason Number Forty-Five: She changed her description of the interior of the house wherein the alleged attack took place.

According to attorney Margot Cleveland, Dr. Ford made many changes to her story, including changes to her description of the interior of the house wherein the party allegedly occurred. Initially she described the stairwell as "short."[41] Later she described the stairwell not as short, but as "narrow." Also, she initially stated that the house contained a combined family room/living room, but later in her testimony she stated the house had a family room that was separate from the living room![42]

These changes may seem trivial, but they are just a few more suspicious changes in her story amidst numerous big changes; therefore, they should not be ignored! And Margot Cleveland points out that in Dr. Ford's story "each change came when the story didn't make sense OR was able to be disproven." (For further details read Margot Cleveland's analysis at *ChicksOn-Right.com*.)[43]

Reason Number Forty-Six: She changed her story regarding the voices she heard immediately after the alleged attack.

She gave contradictory statements about what she heard at the party. In her letter to Senator Feinstein Dr. Ford said that, after the alleged attack had occurred, she heard Brett Kavanaugh and Mark Judge talking to other party attendees downstairs while she was locked in the upstairs bathroom. However, in her testimony to the Senate Judiciary Committee she stated that she could not hear them talking to other people at the party when they were downstairs. Under questioning she said she assumed they were talking to others. John Nolte points out that this is difficult to reconcile given that, "In the Feinstein letter, though, Ford makes it sound as though hearing the conversation downstairs was her signal that it was safe for her to leave the bathroom."[44]

Reason Number Forty-Seven: Many of Dr. Ford's story changes have occurred "at her convenience."

Margot Cleveland, writing in *USAtoday.com*, stated that, "But the problem for Ford is not that she doesn't remember everything: It is that everything she remembers changes at her convenience."

Like others who have studied Dr. Ford's statements, Margot Cleveland noted that she changed the date of the alleged attack from the mid 1980's to the early 1980's; changed the number of party attendees from five (three boys and two girls) to six (four boys and two girls); changed the general location where the party supposedly had taken place; changed a "short" stairwell into a "narrow" stairwell, changed a combined family room /living room into separate rooms, etc.

Margot Cleveland stated that some of the changes in Dr. Ford's statements "are even more significant because in each circumstance Ford altered her story only after Kavanaugh and Senate investigators had obtained evidence to disprove her original tale." As stated earlier, "each change came when the story didn't make sense OR was able to be disproven."

Margot Cleveland, who is an attorney, ended her article by stating, "Open-minded Americans of all stripes should see that – emotions aside – Ford's testimony is completely devoid of credibility:" She added, "Yes, victims must be believed. But Ford is not a victim – at least not of Kavanaugh."[45]

Reason Number Forty-Eight: Many of the important details that Dr. Ford cannot remember are "coincidently convenient."

Matt Walsh of *TheDailyWire.com* is just as skeptical as Margot Cleveland. According to Walsh, "It's not just that Ford can't remember – it's that she specifically can't remember any of the details that might prove or disprove her claim. She also can't remember the things she did and said even in the last few months." Welsh notes that if her memory is so poor, how can she be "100 percent certain" that the person who allegedly attacked her was an adolescent named Brett Kavanaugh?

Walsh added, "But it's more than that. Ford's story has changed to get around Kavanaugh's defenses. These aren't random changes in the narrative. These are targeted and calculated changes." He further noted that her forgetfulness, story gaps, and story changes are all "coincidently convenient." Walsh concluded that, "The coincidences are simply too convenient and too numerous to truly be coincidental." He titled his article, "Walsh: How We Know That Christine Ford Is A Liar."[46]

Reason Number Forty-Nine: Dr. Ford notified reporters and politicians, but not law enforcement, of the alleged attack.

Dr. Ford did not notify her parents nor law enforcement of the alleged assault in the 1980s. Her first report appears to be in 2012 when she spoke to her therapist. Instead of notifying law enforcement, 36 years later she contacted the tip line of the left-wing newspaper, *The Washington Post*, she contacted Democrat lawmakers, and she enlisted the help of Democrat attorneys who are also leftist political activists. Dr. Ford, who is a registered Democrat, is also an anti-Trump marcher! Therefore, it appears her allegation against Judge Kavanaugh was not motivated by a desire to "fight crime" or to protect other women, but to advance a Democrat political agenda.[47]

Reason Number Fifty: Her timing is suspect!

The **timing** of her allegation is separate from, but intimately related to, the above behavior of Dr. Ford. Not only did she notify left-wing politicians, left-wing lawyers, and a left-wing newspaper instead of notifying law enforcement regarding the alleged assault – she waited 36 years to do so!

Why did Dr. Ford not notify her parents or law enforcement of the alleged assault when it occurred? **Why did she wait 36 years?** Dr. Ford waited almost four decades – until she believed Judge Brett Kavanaugh may be nominated to the U.S. Supreme Court by President Trump – before she notified *The Washington Post*, Democrat lawmakers, and politically active left-wing Democrat attorneys. The timing of her actions further suggests she was motivated by a desire to advance a Democrat political agenda, and not a desire to "fight crime" or protect other women.[48]

Reason Number Fifty-One: She claimed ignorance in how to contact the U.S. Senate.

Christine Blasey Ford holds a Ph.D. in psychology, is a professor of psychology at Palo Alto University, and is a researcher at the Stanford University School of Medicine. However, she claimed she did not know how to contact the U.S. Senate, but she did know how to contact her congresswoman, Democrat Anna G. Eshoo.[49, 50]

Janice Fiamengo of the University of Ottawa asked, "What kind of an academic doesn't know how to contact the U.S. Senate to give it information about a Supreme Court nominee? Well, the kind that teaches at Palo Alto University in California." Fiamengo then indicated that, while Dr. Ford said she didn't know how to contact the U.S. Senate, the Facebook page of Palo Alto

University provided that information for students and faculty alike.[51]

Anyone with Internet access and an average IQ can search the web for information on how to contact the U.S. Senate. So why did this highly educated university professor and researcher say she did not know how to perform this simple act? Was this part of her "Damsel in Distress" (feminist proletarian) facade?

Reason Number Fifty-Two: She made a false statement to *The Washington Post!*

Dr. Ford told *The Washington Post* that she was disappointed when Trump defeated Hillary in November of 2016 because Judge Brett Kavanaugh's name was mentioned as a possible nominee for the U.S. Supreme Court. However, Judge Brett Kavanaugh's name was not placed on President Trump's list of possible nominees in 2016. Instead, his name was placed on the list one year later, in November of 2017.[52]

Reason Number Fifty-Three: She provided confusing information regarding her therapy notes and *The Washington Post*.

Rachel Mitchell's report regarding Dr. Ford's testimony before the Senate Judiciary Committee revealed a long series of confusing statements regarding her contact with *The Washington Post* reporter and the sharing of her therapy notes. For example, Dr. Ford could not remember if she shared with the reporter a full or partial set of notes, and she could not remember if she provided actual therapist notes or her summary of the notes. (For a detailed review of the confusing information provided by Dr. Ford regarding this issue visit *Breitbart.com*.)[53]

This is just one of many instances wherein Dr. Ford behaved like a befuddled adolescent who could not recall simple facts regarding her own recent, important activities. This is certainly not the kind of behavior one would expect from a psychology professor and medical researcher.

Reason Number Fifty-Four: She gave conflicting reports regarding the time period wherein she informed her husband of the alleged assault.

Sex crimes expert Rachel Mitchell pointed out that Dr. Ford told *The Washington Post* that she informed her husband of the alleged assault at the beginning of their marriage. However, when she testified before the Senate Judiciary Committee she said she informed her husband of the alleged assault before they were married.[54] Which Dr. Ford story do you believe?

Reason Number Fifty-Five: Dr. Ford's reported desire for anonymity is contradicted by her behavior!

Dr. Ford's claim that she wanted to remain anonymous is contradicted by the fact that she contacted *The Washington Post*, a left-wing newspaper. As Brad Slager of *RedState.com* stated, Dr. Ford's behavior "challenges common sense" because "she approached one of the largest national newspapers with her accusation. To what end? Did she expect it to be reported anonymously and held as proof?"[55]

Reason Number Fifty-Six: She claimed she did not know about the offer to provide private testimony!

During her testimony Dr. Ford indicated that she was confused as to whether or not she could have given her testimony in private, and that U.S. Senate staff members were willing to travel to California to ensure her privacy and address her alleged fear of flying. Either her attorneys kept this vital information from her – or she has an extremely poor memory and could not recall recently receiving this critically important information.

There is a third, alternative explanation: She may have been lying! Given the numerous refuted and contradicted statements provided by Dr. Ford, this is a reasonable conclusion.

As reported by Lorie Byrd of *Townhall.com*, "For Ford's lawyers to keep the Committee's offer from her, would not only require them to decide to withhold it, but to also keep her away from all news, and from anyone who watched or read the news. If the lawyers did withhold that offer from Ford, they not only committed malpractice, but they viciously duped her into reliving the moment she said had ruined her life. And duped her into reliving it in the most public way possible. And they told her it was the Republicans' fault.

"If that happened, that is **evil**. And it would be proof that the Democrats on the Committee, or at the very least her Democrat lawyers, got what they wanted all along – a televised #MeToo moment that would not only destroy a Supreme Court nomination, but serve as a club to bludgeon Republicans with in the midterms. And they didn't mind using a woman who claims to be a sexual assault victim to do it."[56]

In other words, it is possible, but unlikely, that her attorneys failed to inform her of the option to give her testimony in private and in California. Her attorneys would have committed malpractice for withholding that information from her. Thus, it is more likely that she lied under oath or was so confused that she could not think clearly.

Judicial Watch has placed Dr. Ford and her attorneys in a precarious position. According to Joshua Paladino of *Liberty-Headlines.com*, Judicial Watch "submitted a bar complaint against Dr. Christine Blasey Ford's lawyers 'for violating the rules of professional responsibility in their representation' by withholding crucial information."[57] So, her attorney's may be forced to admit that they violated the District of Columbia Rules of Professional Conduct by not informing Dr. Ford about the offer to interview her in private in California, or they may be forced to admit that Dr. Ford lied under oath or was confused when she indicated she was unaware that such an offer had been made by Senator Chuck Grassley, the Chairman of the Senate Judicial Committee. Time will tell – maybe!

Reason Number Fifty-Seven: She changed her story about how she obtained her attorneys!

Dr. Ford had initially claimed that her attorneys were recommended to her by her friends, but later she changed her story and acknowledged that her attorneys were recommended by Senator Feinstein's office.[58]

Which Dr. Ford do you believe, the one who said her attorneys were recommended to her by her friends, or the one who said they were recommended by Senator's Feinstein's office?

Reason Number Fifty-Eight: Senator Diane Feinstein initially withheld Dr. Ford's letter from the Senate Judiciary Committee because she knew her allegation was implausible!

Prior to the hearings, Judge Brett Kavanaugh was personally interviewed by many senators, including Democrat Senator Diane Feinstein. Senator Feinstein received Dr. Ford's letter which was dated July 30, 2018, and she interviewed Judge Kavanaugh on August 20, 2018. So, given that Senator Feinstein received the letter from Dr. Ford many weeks before she interviewed Judge Kavanaugh, why did she not question him in their private meeting about the alleged sexual assault? Why did she wait until the hearings were concluding and senators were on the verge of voting to confirm (or to not confirm) Judge Kavanaugh?

In an interviewer with a *Fox News* reporter, Senator Feinstein said, "I can't say everything is truthful" in Dr. Ford's letter.[59] Later she tried to walk back that eye-opening statement.

Reportedly, Dr. Ford did not want to go public with her allegation, but someone leaked the contents of the letter, and Senator Feinstein and her staff cannot be dismissed as suspects. Former Speaker of the House Republican Newt Gingrich stated on *Fox News* that Democrat Senator Feinstein "was once a responsible and honorable person," implying that she no longer demonstrates those attributes.[60]

It certainly appears as though Senator Feinstein initially withheld Dr. Ford's letter because she knew the allegation against Judge Kavanaugh was implausible. However, with the senate on the verge of voting, and the midterm election on the horizon, producing the letter at the last minute would certainly disrupt and delay the proceedings. With a lot of help from their friends in the Democrat media, perhaps the proceedings could be delayed beyond the midterm election when – hopefully for Feinstein – Democrats would take control of the U.S. Senate and the Senate Judiciary Committee. They could thus prevent President Trump and the Republicans from placing a second constitutionalist on the U.S. Supreme Court.

Reason Number Fifty-Nine: Dr. Ford's attorneys made many ridiculous demands, indicating they knew her allegation was implausible.

Dr. Ford and her attorneys made many demands before agreeing to testify before the Senate Judiciary Committee.[61] For example, they wanted no questions from lawyers, only from members of the Senate Judiciary Committee. They wanted Mark Judge, Brett Kavanaugh's high school friend and alleged accomplice, to be subpoenaed to testify. They also wanted an additional and extensive FBI background check on Judge Brett Kavanaugh.

Furthermore, they wanted Judge Brett Kavanaugh to not be present in the room to face his accuser – as traditionally occurs in American courtrooms. Any honest person must ask, if Dr. Ford was telling the truth, why was she afraid to tell the truth in front of Judge Brett Kavanaugh? Under oath Dr. Ford testified that she was "100 percent" sure that an adolescent boy named Brett Kavanaugh had attacked her, so why was she afraid to have him hear her speak the truth? Moreover, they wanted Judge Brett Kavanaugh to testify BEFORE his accuser testified, not AFTER his accuser, as traditionally occurs in American courtrooms.

These last two demands turn American jurisprudence upside down. In America every person accused of a crime (And yes, sexual assault is a crime.) is given the opportunity to face his or her accuser. However, as requested, Judge Brett Kavanaugh was not present in the room when Dr. Ford testified. In addition, it is absurd to request that the accused testify BEFORE hearing the statements made by his or her accuser! Understandably, this last and most absurd request was not granted.

Finally, in a letter to the Senator Chuck Grassley, one of Dr. Ford's attorneys objected to bringing in an "experienced sex crimes prosecutor" to question Dr. Ford on behalf of Republican Senators. According to attorney Michael R. Bromwich, "This is not a criminal trial for which the involvement of an experienced sex crimes prosecutor would be appropriate. Neither Dr. Blasey Ford nor Judge Kavanaugh is on trial. The goal should be to develop relevant facts, not try a case." He also asked Chairman Grassley to "Please identify this person and ask your staff to send us her resume immediately."[62]

Certainly, attorneys wish to create a climate most favorable for their clients. However, some of the demands made by Dr. Ford's attorneys were ridiculous. This indicates that they knew Dr. Ford's case was not just weak, but implausible when presented to any objective observer! For that reason they needed to twist and bend traditional methods of testimony to make the incredible appear at least semi-credible!

Reason Number Sixty: Judge Brett Kavanaugh has no history or pattern of sexual misconduct!

Sexual predators tend to display a pattern of predatory behavior over a long period of time, such as has been documented for Bill Clinton, Ted Kennedy, Bill Cosby, and Harvey Weinstein, to name just a few beloved, predatory Democrats. No such pattern has been noted for Judge Brett Kavanaugh. There were attempts by leftists to establish a pattern of sexual misconduct by Judge Brett Kavanaugh, but they turned out to be without merit. By contrast, 65 women who have known him in one capacity or another, have signed a letter testifying to his integrity and respect for women, as noted below.

Reason Number Sixty-One: 65 women signed a letter praising Judge Brett Kavanaugh for his respectful treatment of women.

Sixty-five women who have known Judge Brett Kavanaugh from his high school years signed a letter that contained the words "honorably" "respect," "integrity," and "decency" in describing their personal knowledge of, and personal experiences with, Judge Kavanaugh over a period of more than 35 years. So, the pattern of behavior towards women established by Judge Brett Kavanaugh over a period of nearly four decades contradicts the behavior alleged by Dr. Ford and is in stark contrast to that of a sexual predator. His lifelong behavior has been precisely the opposite of what one would expect from a sexual predator!

The signed letter from the 65 women is as follows:

"Dear Chairman Grassley and Ranking Member Feinstein,

"We are women who have known Brett Kavanaugh for more than 35 years and knew him while he attended high school between 1979 and 1983. For the entire time we have known Brett Kavanaugh, he has behaved honorably and treated women with respect. We strongly believe it is important to convey this information to the Committee at this time.

"Brett attended Georgetown Prep, an all-boys high school in Rockville, Maryland. He was an outstanding student and athlete with a wide circle of friends. Almost all of us attended all-girls high schools in the area. We knew Brett well through social events, sports, church and various other activities. Many of us have remained close friends with him and his family over the years. Through the more than 35 years we have known him, Brett has stood out for his friendship, character and integrity. In particular, he has always treated women with decency and respect. That was true when he was in high school, and it has remained true to this day.

"The signers of this letter hold a broad range of political views. Many of us are not lawyers, but we know Brett Kavanaugh as a person. And he has always been a good person."[63]

Reason Number Sixty-Two: The FBI found no evidence of misconduct by Judge Brett Kavanaugh – as an adolescent or as an adult!

Judge Brett Kavanaugh survived six FBI background checks over a period of many years before being accused of assault by Dr. Ford. And he survived a seventh FBI investigation as well, which occurred as a result of Dr. Ford's allegation against him. The

Federal Bureau of Investigation, which is considered a premier investigative body, found no personal or professional misconduct on the part of Judge Brett Kavanaugh at any time in his life.

On October 6, 2018, **Judge** Brett Kavanaugh became **Justice** Brett Kavanaugh. Nearly one month later, on November 3, 2018, the FBI released a final report on its full investigation into all the allegations of sexual misconduct made against him. The FBI interviewed more than 40 individuals, including former classmates, friends, or anyone who may have had any information regarding the allegations made against him. Its conclusion: The FBI could find no evidence to support any of the claims of sexual misconduct lodged against Judge Brett Kavanaugh. Period![64]

Reason Number Sixty-Three: The ABA found no evidence of misconduct by Judge Brett Kavanaugh!

The American Bar Association (ABA) has a reputation for displaying a pro-leftist bias in assessing the qualification of lawyers and judges to serve on the U.S. Supreme Court. However, despite this perceived bias, Judge Brett Kavanaugh received a unanimous rating of "Well-qualified" by the ABA, which is the highest rating one can receive.

In addition, quoting from the assessment of Judge Brett Kavanaugh submitted by the American Bar Association, Senator Lindsey Graham noted the following: "His integrity is absolutely unquestioned. He is very circumspect in his personal conduct, harbors no biases or prejudices, he is entirely ethical, is a really decent person. He is warm, friendly, unassuming. He's the nicest person."[65]

Read the above paragraph to yourself several times, then contrast the ABA's assessment of Judge Brett Kavanaugh to the allegation presented by Dr. Christine Blasey Ford.

Reason Number Sixty-Four: The Senate Judiciary Committee found no evidence of misconduct by Judge Brett Kavanaugh – as an adolescent or as an adult!

On November 3, 2018, the Senate Judiciary Committee released a 414-page document that detailed the findings of its extensive investigation into all of the allegations of sexual misconduct made against Judge Kavanaugh. The actual report is 28 pages long with 386 pages of supporting documents. The bottom line is this: No evidence was found to support any of the numerous allegations made by any of Judge Brett Kavanaugh's accusers. As noted at *Breitbart.com,* the report contained the following:

"After an extensive investigation that included the thorough review of all potentially credible evidence submitted and interviews of more than 40 individuals with information relating to the allegations, including classmates and friends of all those involved, Committee investigators found no witness who could provide any verifiable evidence to support any of the allegations brought against Justice Kavanaugh. In other words, following the separate and extensive investigations by both the Committee and the FBI, there was no evidence to substantiate any of the claims of sexual assault made against Justice Kavanaugh."[66]

Byron York of *Townhall.com* noted that the Senate Judiciary Committee investigated every plausible and every implausible allegation made against Judge Kavanaugh.[67]

Regarding the allegation made by Dr. Christine Blasey Ford who claimed that a drunken 17-year-old Brett Kavanaugh attempted to rape her 36 years ago at a party when she was 15 years old,

"Committee investigators found no verifiable evidence that supported Dr. Ford's allegation against Judge Kavanaugh."

Deborah Ramirez claimed that 35 years ago an intoxicated Brett Kavanaugh exposed himself to her at a party when she a student at Yale. Once again,

"The committee found no verifiable evidence to support Ramirez's allegations."

Julie Swetnick alleged that a young Brett Kavanaugh, along with other boys, spiked punch at high school parties 36 years ago. When the girls became easy prey, they were gang-raped, and Brett Kavanaugh was a party member. Regarding this horrendous claim,

"The committee found no verifiable evidence to support Swetnick's allegations."

An anonymous accuser claimed that in 1985 both Judge Brett Kavanaugh and his friend Mark Judge sexually assaulted a woman on a boat. In response to this claim that was reportedly made from Rhode Island,

"The committee found no verifiable evidence to support the allegations" of this anonymous accuser.

Another anonymous accuser claimed that in 1998 Judge Brett Kavanaugh "very aggressively and sexually" shoved a woman that he was dating at that time. This second anonymous accuser was reportedly from Colorado. In the report we find the following:

"The committee found no evidence to support the allegations in the anonymous Colorado letter."

Lastly, another anonymous accuser labeled as a "Jane Doe" alleged that, in a time and place that was not specified, Judge

Brett Kavanaugh struck her and forced her to perform oral sex. In addition she claimed that he and another man raped her "several times." Once again, Senate Judiciary Committee Chairman Senator Chuck Grassley wrote,

"The committee found no evidence to support the allegations in the Jane Doe letter."

Senator Chuck Grassley rightly believes that committee investigators had been sent on numerous, time-consuming and expensive "wild goose chases" (those are my words, not his). To discourage this from occurring again he has asked the Justice Department to investigate some of the women, including attorney Michael Avenatti, who represented Julie Swetnick.

Before moving on to Reason Number Sixty-Five, pause for a few moments and consider the following:

Judge Brett Kavanaugh was made aware of all the above allegations lodged against him, whether they were conceivable or ridiculous! Put yourself in his shoes for a few minutes. Just as the Senate is about to vote on your confirmation to the U.S. Supreme Court, a half-dozen people of the opposite sex – who you have never met – claim that you sexually assaulted them!

Suddenly, Democrat Senators are calling you "evil," and they also make the unprecedented, lynch mob-style claim that you do not have the presumption of innocence until proven guilty. Instead of seeking the truth, the corrupt leftist media repeatedly slant the news to make you appear guilty when there is no evidence of wrongdoing on your part. Your life is now being threatened, and the life of your spouse is threatened. Not only is your confirmation in peril, but your reputation has been forever tarnished and your entire career is now in jeopardy! Decades of hard work and careful planning have been destroyed – almost overnight!

When publically addressing these allegations on national television (with more than 20 million viewers), would you maintain a "judicial temperament?" If you did, you would be found guilty in the court of public opinion, and public opinion most certainly sways political opinion! And those judges, lawyers, law professors, politicians, and others who claim that Judge Kavanaugh should have been rejected because of his impassioned defense – know very well that it was the only way he could have delivered a successful defense! How sad!

Reason Number Sixty-Five: The Clinton Smear Machine found no evidence of misconduct by Judge Brett Kavanaugh – as an adolescent or as an adult!

Before becoming a judge, Brett Kavanaugh worked under Ken Starr during the impeachment of President Bill Clinton. At that time the Clinton Smear Machine counter investigated Ken Starr, Brett Kavanaugh and others who were investigating Bill Clinton. As Judge Brett Kavanaugh noted in his opening statement to the Senate Judiciary Committee, the Clinton Smear Machine found no wrongdoing by him – even though a leftist offered $1 million for any evidence of sexual misconduct. So, just like the FBI, the ABA, the Senate Judiciary Committee, and others listed below, the Clinton Smear Machine found no evidence of misconduct by Judge Brett Kavanaugh, sexual or otherwise![68, 69]

Reason Number Sixty-Six: The Democrat Senatorial Smear Machine and its supporters produced no credible evidence of misconduct by Judge Brett Kavanaugh!

With millions of dollars at their disposal, the highly motivated and corrupt Democrat Senatorial Smear Machine produced transparent theatrics, but generated no credible evidence of misconduct by Judge Brett Kavanaugh – as an adolescent or as an adult! Instead, they produced negative and fake statements to smear an innocent man.

Senator Lindsey Graham said to Judge Kavanaugh, "...on July 9th, the day you were nominated to the Supreme Court by President Trump, [Democrat] Senator Schumer said, 23 minutes after your nomination, 'I will oppose Judge Kavanaugh's nomination with everything I have. I hope a bipartisan majority will do the same. The stakes are simply too high for anything less.'"[70]

So, when Democrat Senator Chuck Schumer said "I will oppose Judge Kavanaugh's nomination with everything I have," he meant everything, including a vicious, unprecedented character assassination of a man described by the American Bar Association (again) as follows: "His integrity is absolutely unquestioned. He is very circumspect in his personal conduct, harbors no biases or prejudices, he is entirely ethical, is a really decent person. He is warm, friendly, unassuming. He's the nicest person."

As noted in Chapter Two, Democrat Senator Cory Booker stated that those who support the elevation of Judge Brett Kavanaugh to the U.S. Supreme Court are "complicit in evil," thus inferring that Judge Brett Kavanaugh is an "evil" person. Senator Richard "Stolen Valor" Blumenthal, a Democrat, said "Judge Kavanaugh is your worst nightmare."

In addition, Democrat Senator Elizabeth "Pocahontas" Warren said Judge Brett Kavanaugh's "nomination is a threat to people of color, to women, to workers, to the LGBTQ community, to people living in poverty." Democrat Senator Kamala Harris stated that, with the nomination of Judge Kavanaugh, "We're looking at a destruction of the Constitution of the United States." Democrat Senator Jeff Merkley said, "This is a nominee who wants to pave the path to tyranny." Democrat Terry McAuliffe, the former Governor of Virginia, said, "The nomination of Judge Brett Kavanaugh will threaten the lives of millions of Americans for decades to come."[71]

Therefore, it appears that Brad Slager of *RedState.com* was correct when he said, "The disgust and outrage at this fiasco of **character assassination** should not be targeted at Dr. Ford. She is only a tool in this, wielded by a venal and corrupt body within the Democratic Party."[72]

So, although Senate Judiciary Committee Democrats conducted a "search and destroy" campaign against Judge Brett Kavanaugh and assassinated his character, they produced zero evidence to support any of the allegations launched against him! They produced zero evidence to demonstrate that the numerous investigations conducted by the FBI, the ABA, and the Senate Judiciary Committee could be credibly challenged!

Reason Number Sixty-Seven: The Democrat Media Smear Machine produced no credible evidence of misconduct by Judge Brett Kavanaugh!

With thousands of highly motivated and corrupt reporters, investigative journalists, researchers, and writers at their disposal, the corrupt Democrat Media Smear Machine produced no credible evidence of misconduct by Judge Brett Kavanaugh – as an adolescent or as an adult! Instead, they produced uncorroborated, unverifiable, negative, and fake news reports to smear an innocent man!

Consider the following quotes:

"Broadcasters grant only 4% of Brett Kavanaugh news coverage to judge's side of story: Study." – Jennifer Harper, *Washington-Times.com*, September 26, 2018[73]

"The Media Research Center says that 90 percent of the news coverage has been negative toward Kavanaugh. Honestly, I'm surprised it's that low. It looks like 99.9 percent to me." – Mark Levin, *Life, Liberty & Levin,* October 7, 2018[74]

"*NBC News* deliberately hid vital information that would have helped clear Brett Kavanaugh of the serial rape allegations Julie Swetnick and her attorney, Michael Avenatti, leveled against him." – John Nolte, *Breitbart.com*, October 26, 2018[75]

So, despite their corruption and extreme bias against Judge Brett Kavanaugh, the Democrat Media Smear Machine produced no credible evidence of misconduct of any kind by this U.S. Supreme Court nominee. (The extent to which the Democrat Media Smear Machine engaged in relentless character assassination against this innocent man is discussed in detail in Chapter Two: Judge Brett Kavanaugh and the Art of Character Assassination.)

Reason Number Sixty-Eight: Senator Lindsey Graham exposed the treatment of Judge Kavanaugh as an "unethical sham!"

The Republican members of the Senate Judiciary Committee had access to confidential information regarding Judge Kavanaugh that was denied to the general public. The impassioned, out-of-character condemnation of his Democratic colleagues by Senator Lindsey Graham was historic. It could only be displayed by a man who was thoroughly convinced, by all the evidence he had access to, that Judge Brett Kavanaugh was the victim of a vicious character assassination. Nearly all Republican senators voted to confirm Judge Brett Kavanaugh.

Senator Lindsey Graham's short but powerful speech was one of several factors that inspired this writer to seriously investigate the allegation Dr. Christine Blasey Ford launched against Judge Brett Kavanaugh. An impassioned defense was also offered by Judge Brett Kavanaugh, but that was expected if he was to survive this attack on his character and his future.

Senator Lindsey Graham, joined by others who were truly out-raged by the mistreatment of Judge Kavanaugh, turned on his fellow senators. Pointing his finger at his Democrat colleagues he said, speaking of Associate Justices Sonia Sotomayor and Elena Kagan, whom he voted for, "I would never do to them what you have done to this guy! This is the most unethical sham since I've been in politics." Knowing that all Americans did not have access to the same information that he had, Senator Graham said, "I hope the American people can see through this sham."[76]

As previously stated, Senator Lindsey Graham quoted from the assessment of Judge Brett Kavanaugh that was submitted by the American Bar Association. Senator Graham's quote included the following: "His integrity is absolutely unquestioned. He is very circumspect in his personal conduct, harbors no biases or prejudices, he is entirely ethical, is a really decent person. He is warm, friendly, unassuming. He's the nicest person."[77]

The ABA assessment, combined with the results of numerous FBI investigations (which Graham had access to, but was denied to the American public) and the letter of support from 65 women who knew Judge Kavanaugh for more than 35 years, along with the deceitful behavior of his Democrat colleagues, painted a very compelling picture.

In addition, Republican Senator Cory Gardner also received an anonymous letter alleging that Judge Kavanaugh had physically assaulted a woman after leaving a Washington D.C. bar in 1998. According to the letter, "When they left the bar (under the influence of alcohol) they were all shocked when Brett Kavanaugh shoved her friend against the wall very aggressively and sexually."

Judge Kavanaugh noted that "We're dealing with an anonymous letter about an anonymous person and an anonymous friend. It's ridiculous." Of course, he was correct, because nothing in the letter could be verified – not even the identity of the supposed victim or any witnesses.[78] The "unethical sham" Senator Lindsey Graham spoke of was obvious to Judge Kavanaugh as well!

Most disturbingly, all of these allegations were presented to Senator Chuck Grassley, the Chairman of the Judiciary Committee, AFTER senators had finished personally interviewing Judge Kavanaugh in individual sessions; AFTER senators had finished questioning Judge Kavanaugh in open hearings, and AFTER it appeared Judge Kavanaugh would be confirmed to sit on the U.S. Supreme Court because nothing could be found to disqualify him – even after six FBI investigations into his private and professional life.

Reason Number Sixty-Nine: Judge Kavanaugh's refutation was thoroughly convincing!

Judge Brett Kavanaugh gave one of the most convincing defensive speeches in American history – shattering Dr. Ford's allegation and exposing the Democrats "search and destroy" tactics that replaced the "advice and consent" role of the U.S. Senate.

Consider the following five quotes:

One: "I don't think I've ever felt more strongly about something that's happening politically than I do about this. I can't tell you why this is affecting me so much, so deeply, I mean, **I feel physically ill over all of this.**

"Watching his [Judge Kavanaugh's] testimony yesterday, I was crying like a baby. I don't know if it's because I see in him every good man that I know and I just can't – I cannot fathom living in

54

a world in which my husband or my brothers or my dad could be [charged] with something like rape and not be presumed innocent until proven guilty." – Allie Beth Stuckey, Reported by Beth Baumann, *Townhall.com,* September 30, 2018[79]

Two: "Judge Kavanaugh showed America exactly why I nominated him. **His testimony was powerful, honest, and riveting**. Democrats' search and destroy strategy is disgraceful and this process has been a total sham, an effort to delay, obstruct, and resist. The Senate must vote!" – President Donald Trump, September 27, 2018 Tweet[80]

Three: "Judge Brett Kavanaugh's defense will go down in history as **one of the most compelling and consequential speeches of our time.** The emotional impact of his righteous indignation was raw and riveting. The pain on his and his family's faces was agony to watch." – Janice Shaw Crouse, *AmericanThinker.com,* September 29, 2018[81]

Four: "His [Judge Brett Kavanaugh's] defiant September 27 statement denying the charges leveled against him in the course of his Supreme Court confirmation **is the defining speech of our time.**" – Christopher Caldwell, *WeeklyStandard.com,* October 5, 2018[82]

Five: Judge Brett Kavanaugh's defensive speech **"...changed the course of American history."** – Kyle Smith, *NationalReview.com,* September 28, 2018[83]

(Reminder: As stated earlier in the Important Introductory Notes, with the exception of some news headlines, **all bold lettering** in this book was added by this author, and not by the original authors of any quoted material. That includes the above five quotes.)

Why did his speech change the course of American history? Because without that impassioned and well-reasoned speech, someone other than Judge Brett Kavanaugh would have filled the vacancy created by the retirement of Associate Justice Anthony Kennedy! Before he made that speech his chances of becoming a U.S. Supreme Court Associate Justice were next to zero.

Dr. Christine Blasey Ford presented a seemingly convincing allegation to the Senate Judiciary Committee and the viewing public. Although there were many obvious holes in her testimony, her nervous, insecure body language combined with her childlike voice, overshadowed those weaknesses. After little Chrissy "Damsel in Distress" Ford completed her testimony, the confirmation of Judge Brett Kavanaugh appeared to be – not just in jeopardy, but stone cold dead!

But Judge Brett Kavanaugh worked a miracle!

When I stated that Judge Kavanaugh shattered Dr. Ford allegation, I was referring to the first few paragraphs of his opening statement on September 27, 2018, which are found below (and also on page four of this book):

"Less than two weeks ago, Dr. Ford publicly accused me of committing wrongdoing at an event more than 36 years ago when we were both in high school. I denied the allegation immediately, categorically and unequivocally. All four people allegedly at the event, including Dr. Ford's longtime friend, Ms. Keyser, have said they recall no such event. Her longtime friend, Ms. Keyser, said under penalty of felony that she does not know me, and does not believe she ever saw me at a party, ever.

"Here is the quote from Ms. Keyser's attorney's letter: quote, 'Simply put, Ms. Keyser does not know Mr. Kavanaugh, and she has no recollection of ever being at a party or gathering where he was present, with or without Dr. Ford,' end quote. Think about that fact.

"The day after the allegation appeared, I told this committee that I wanted a hearing as soon as possible to clear my name. I demanded a hearing for the very next day. Unfortunately, it took the committee 10 days to get to this hearing. In those 10 long days, as was predictable, and as I predicted, my family and my name have been totally and permanently destroyed by vicious and false additional accusations. The 10-day delay has been harmful to me and my family, to the Supreme Court and to the country."[84]

By immediately pointing out that all four party attendees listed by Dr. Ford failed to support her claims, Judge Brett Kavanaugh demonstrated beyond all doubt that Dr. Ford must be either dishonest, delusional, seriously confused, memory impaired, or some combination thereof!

Reason Number Seventy: Her parents failed to publicly support her!

Along with the support of his wife and daughters, Judge Brett Kavanaugh also received strong public support from his father and mother during this stressful period. Writers have reported that, during the confirmation hearings, Judge Brett Kavanaugh's mother was seen wiping tears from her eyes as he spoke fondly of his parents.[85]

At this point, you, the reader, may say to yourself, "Of course Judge Brett Kavanaugh received support from his parents. That would be expected." If that is your conclusion, how do you explain the absence of Dr. Ford's parents and two brothers?

While Judge Kavanaugh received strong public support from his parents, Dr. Ford's parents and two brothers were missing in action. Matt Vespa wrote in *Townhall.com* that "Her family has been conspicuously absent in this ordeal."[86]

Dr. Ford received many letters of support, including one from one-half of her family. However, the family support letter was signed only by members from her husband's side of the family. The family support letter did not include the signatures of Dr. Ford's father, mother, or her two brothers.

Dr. Ford's parents are registered Republicans, just as Judge Kavanaugh's parents are registered Republicans. However, Dr. Ford is a registered Democrat and an anti-Trump marcher. Dr. Ford's husband, Russell Ford, stated that, "She didn't always get along with her parents because of differing political views." He also stated that his wife relocated to California in part to escape "the D.C. scene."[87]

Clearly, Judge Kavanaugh received solid public support from his parents because he was undergoing an enormously stressful period in his life. But so was Dr. Ford! In her opening statement to the Senate Judiciary Committee she said "I am here today not because I want to be. I am terrified. I am here because I believe it is my civic duty."[88]

Given that she was facing a terrifying ordeal, why did her parents not support her publicly as we saw with the parents of Judge Kavanaugh? Both sets of parents live within a reasonable distance from Washington, D.C. where the hearings were conducted. Both families had received threats, so both families could have used fear as an excuse to distance themselves from this process. But neither set of parents stated that fear entered into their decision-making.

We can only speculate, but we know that Dr. Ford has provided false or conflicting statements on numerous occasions through-out this process. Therefore, could it be that her parents did not find her to be credible – and therefore they did not want to back what they believed to be an obvious instance, or possible instance, of politically-motivated character assassination?

This is an assumption, and it could not stand alone. But it is a reasonable assumption based on all that has been uncovered, and therefore it will be included as another reason to question the veracity of Dr. Ford's allegation against Judge Kavanaugh.

Given that Dr. Ford did not receive public support from close blood relatives who have an intimate understanding of her character, why should she expect public support from truth-seeking strangers? Why should she expect support from truth-seeking members of the Senate Judiciary Committee? Why should she expect public support from any truth-seeking Ameri-can who is aware of 5, 10, or more of the 80 Reasons outlined in this book?

Reason Number Seventy-One: A sex crimes expert found Dr. Ford's allegation lacks evidence!

In her report regarding the testimony provided by Dr. Ford, sex crimes expert Rachel Mitchell concluded that "In the legal context, here is my bottom line. A 'he said, she said' case is incredibly difficult to prove. But this case is even weaker than that. I do not think that a reasonable prosecutor would bring this case based on the evidence." This veteran prosecutor and sex crimes expert also stated that, "Nor do I believe that this evidence is sufficient to satisfy the preponderance-of-the-evidence standard." According to John Nolte of *Breitbart.com*, "This means Ford's story does not reach the 50-50 level of being more likely to have occurred than not."[89]

Reason Number Seventy-Two: A sex crimes expert found Dr. Ford's reported academic problems to be rather suspicious.

According to sex crimes investigator Rachel Mitchell, Dr. Ford claims that, as a result of the alleged sexual assault, "She alleges that she struggled academically in college, but she has never made any similar claim about her last two years of high school." As Ben Sellers of *LibertyHeadlines.com* has noted, "Mitchell also points out Ford's vague accounts of the impact that the alleged trauma had, claiming that it caused her to do poorly her first two years at the University of North Carolina – but clearly not so poorly in her final years of high school that she was unable to gain entry to the selective school."[90]

So, based on Dr. Ford's testimony, the alleged assault had little or no immediate impact on her high school academic performance, but did negatively affect her later college academic performance. But this is precisely the opposite of what one would expect! One would expect a significant negative academic impact immediately after the alleged assault, which would lessen over time after she entered college.

Reason Number Seventy-Three: She has demonstrated an exceedingly poor memory for both recent and past events.

Phillip Klein of the *WashingtonExaminer.com* quoted from the report provided by veteran sex crimes investigator Rachel Mitchell who stated the following: "Dr. Ford has struggled to recall important recent events relating to her allegations, and her testimony regarding recent events raises further questions about her memory."[91]

According to Phillip Klein, "This is, perhaps, the most damning of all. Her patchy memory from 36 years ago could be chalked up to the odd way that trauma affects individuals, allowing her to recall certain details with confidence while forgetting others. But her failure to recall significant details of interactions that happened over the past few weeks or months is damning."

Klein also noted that Rachel Mitchell stated that, "Dr. Ford could not remember if she showed a full or partial set of therapy notes to *The Washington Post* reporter." Dr. Ford also "does not remember if she actually had a copy of the notes" when she contacted *The Washington Post*. Moreover, Dr. Ford was confused about when she took the polygraph test, and was not sure if she took the exam the day of her grandmother's funeral. It must be noted that she testified in September, and took the polygraph exam just one month earlier!

While under oath, Dr. Ford claimed that she was "100 percent certain" that the person who physically assaulted her 36 years ago at a party was 17-year-old Brett Kavanaugh. But she has demonstrated a profound loss of memory for both past and recent events. She has no memory, or a mistaken memory, about numerous important facts regarding the alleged assault. So, how can she be "100 percent certain" that Brett Kavanaugh assaulted her almost four decades ago when she has been 100 percent confused on numerous, critically important issues – both past and recent?

Reason Number Seventy-Four: We cannot trust the accuracy of Dr. Ford's testimony because Dr. Ford did not trust the accuracy of her testimony.

As noted by Brad Slager of *RedState.com*, "Early in the cross examination Dr. Ford was asked if the letter she had submitted to the committee was accurate." However, instead of answering "Yes" to the question – as one would expect, she asked to see the letter. The letter was supposedly written by her in preparation for her testimony. If she was a perfectly honest individual she would have been fully confident that the letter she prepared was accurate and there would be no need to review it once again.

According to Brad Slager, "Her desire to look over the letter once again to determine it was accurate enough to be entered into the record is revealing. This indicates it likely was crafted, or created with a committee of some sort, and she wanted to be sure elements would not be pulled out as possibly leading to a perjury charge. A victim detailing her honest account should have no need to clarify her writing."[92]

Reason Number Seventy-Five: All charges were immediately dropped against Judge Kavanaugh when he became Associate Justice Kavanaugh!

Immediately after Judge Brett Kavanaugh was sworn in as an Associate Justice of the U.S. Supreme Court, Dr. Ford and her attorneys drop all charges against Justice Brett Kavanaugh and asked that all investigations cease.

In addition, Dr. Ford's attorneys stated that, if Democrats gain control of the House of Representatives in the future (which they did) and impeachment proceedings are brought against Associate Justice Brett Kavanaugh, Dr. Ford would not partici-pate in that effort to remove him from the bench![93, 94, 95]

If Dr. Ford believed it was her "civic duty" to prevent Judge Brett Kavanaugh from being elevated to the U.S. Supreme Court, why does she not believe it is her civic duty to remove Justice Brett Kavanaugh from the U.S. Supreme Court?

This public process has exposed Dr. Ford as an individual who is habitually deceitful, often confused, delusional, or severely memory impaired – or some mixture thereof. Dr. Ford and her attorneys know that continuing this process would expose them to additional public scrutiny, and thus further unmask them as untrustworthy political activists and not as credible "crime fighters" or defenders of women!

Reason Number Seventy-Six: It is obvious to any objective, truth-seeking observer, that Dr. Christine Blasey Ford is simply not credible based on her strikingly incongruent behavior!

Actually, to say that Dr. Ford is not credible – is a profound understatement!

"Open-minded Americans of all stripes should see that – emotions aside – Ford's testimony is completely devoid of credibility:" – Margot Cleveland, Attorney at Law[96]

The television appearance of a profoundly befuddled, ignorant, and memory impaired "Damsel in Distress" with the voice of a frightened 15-year-old girl did not match the resume of a highly educated 51-year-old professional woman.

It is incomprehensible that a woman who possesses a bachelor's degree, two master's degrees, and a doctorate degree from highly respected universities; who works as a professor at Palo Alto University; who works as a researcher at the Stanford University School of Medicine; and who is a published author in academic areas that require meticulous attention to detail, could be so profoundly befuddled, ignorant, and memory impaired regarding her allegation against Judge Brett Kavanaugh – and regarding critically important recent events! We have all heard about the fictional or the stereotypical "absent-minded professor," but this is ridiculous! This is simply not plausible!

As stated elsewhere in this book, Dr. Ford earned a master's degree in epidemiology from the Stanford University School of Medicine. She focused on biostatistics. Dr. Ford also worked as the director of biostatistics at a pharmaceutical company called Corcept Therapeutics, and she collaborated with FDA statisticians. In addition, Dr. Ford has expertise in designing statistical models for research projects. As professional researchers know, a faulty design will lead to faulty conclusions, therefore great care is needed during construction.

So, Dr. Ford works in the complex field of biostatistics and she designs statistical research models to ensure accurate outcomes. To be successful in these areas requires enormous attention to detail; it demands great specificity. To become a published author also requires great attention to detail. So why did she so often demonstrate confused thinking, absent mindedness, and inattention to detail regarding her allegation against Judge Brett Kavanaugh?

Are there two Christine Blasey Fords inhabiting one body, one who is a meticulous professional researcher and author, and the other a confused, delusional, forgetful teenage girl? Is she a "Virtual Manchurian Candidate?" (See Chapter Two, page 102, for a detailed discussion of this topic.)

In addition to this inexplicable "dual personality" type behavior, it was noted earlier that Dr. Ford said Mark Judge attended the party in question, but he refuted her claim. She said Patrick J. Smyth attended the party, but he refuted her claim. She said Leland Ingham Keyser attended the party, but she refuted her claim. She said Brett Kavanaugh attended the party, but he refuted her claim. She said six people attended the party in question, but the letter she sent to Senator Feinstein refuted her own claim.

Dr. Ford said she was claustrophobic, but her behavior and her former boyfriend refuted that claim. She said she had a fear of flying, but her own behavior and her former boyfriend refuted that claim. She said she had no prior knowledge of polygraph testing, but her former boyfriend refuted that claim.

Dr. Ford said the alleged assault by Brett Kavanaugh was recorded in her therapist's notes, but her therapist's notes refuted that claim. She said two boys were involved in the alleged attack, but her therapist's notes refuted that claim. She said she was 15 when the alleged assault took place, but her therapist's notes refuted that claim. She said the alleged assault occurred in the early 1980s, but her therapist's notes refuted that claim. She said her attorneys were recommended by her friends, but she later refuted her own previous claim.

She said Brett Kavanaugh assaulted her, but investigations by the FBI, the ABA, and the Senate Judiciary Committee, in effect, refuted that claim. In addition, given that the character assassins in the Clinton Smear Machine, the Democrat Senatorial Smear Machine, and the Democrat Media Smear Machine produced no evidence to support her claim, they too, in effect, refuted her claim. (I don't know about you, but I detect a pattern here!)

Reason Number Seventy-Seven: Throughout her adult life Dr. Ford has been indoctrinated by a leftist media that encourages a Marxist-style victimhood mentality by making heroes and heroines of "proletarians" who file false, malicious accusations against innocent "bourgeois" males who Hillary Clinton and other leftists smear as "racist, sexist, homophobic, xenophobic, Islamophobic, you name it." (Hillary's Basket of Deplorables!)[97]

Keep in mind that Reason Number Seventy-Seven does not provide evidence that Dr. Ford lied, it simply exposes a context in which lying is generously rewarded in the leftist media world from which the feminist proletariat receive much of their news and information. Like each individual reason, Reason Number Seventy-Seven must be viewed within the context of all the other reasons.

The pervasiveness of false allegations launched against those who symbolize middle class "bourgeois" values is discussed in detail in Chapter Two. To avoid redundancy, only one example will be provided here. Perhaps one of the best examples that epitomizes the generous rewarding of those who launch false, malicious allegations against innocent people who represent so-called "white privilege" or the bourgeoisie takes us back to the 1987 Tawana Brawley case that was defended by Al Sharpton, who was an obscure individual at that time.

The Lie That Made Al Sharpton Famous!

At *GOPUSA.com* there is an article with the following title: "The Mysterious Case of Tawana Brawley' goes in-depth on the lie that made Al Sharpton famous."[98] From this and various other sources we find ample information to reconstruct a very disturbing story from our recent past:

Al Sharpton is not only a Baptist minister and civil rights activist, today he is also a television and movie star! He has made more than a dozen television and motion picture appearances, often playing himself as the "Reverend Al Sharpton."[99] His on-screen adventures at this point in time include the following televisions shows and movies: *Star, Saturday Night Live, Empire, Madea Goes to Jail, Girlfriends, Boston Legal, My Wife and Kids, Holla, Mr. Deeds, Bamboozled, Law & Order: Special Victims Unit, Cold Feet, and Malcolm X.* Also, for years he has hosted his own radio program as well as a cable television show on MSNBC called *Politics Nation With Al Sharpton.*[100]

How did Al Sharpton become so popular and famous with his leftist fans and admirers? As noted earlier, it all started in 1987 when he defended New Yorker Tawana Brawley, a 15-year-old black girl who had **falsely** claimed that she had been abducted, abused, and repeatedly gang-raped by several white men, one of whom wore a badge.

The police were suspicious of Ms. Brawley's claim for many obvious reasons. Firstly, she had been missing for four days, and claimed she had been held outside against her will in a wooded area. But she showed no signs of hypothermia even though outside temperatures were often in the freezing range. The racial slurs of "KKK," "ni**er," and "bitch" were scribbled upside-down on her torso, indicating that she was the author as well as the recipient of those slurs. Perhaps most importantly, no evidence of rape was detected when a rape kit was employed. Also, a witness reported seeing Tawana Brawley crawl into a garbage bag herself – and therefore she was not forced into the bag by her alleged assailants as she had claimed.[101]

To show their solidarity with accuser Anita Hill, in 1991 a full-page advertisement in *The New York Times* contained the names of 1,600 black female supporters. In September, 2018, 1,600 fact-phobic males took out a similar full-page ad in the same newspaper with a banner message that said, "We believe Anita Hill. We also believe Christine Blasey Ford."[102] Likewise, in 1987 the supporters of Tawana Brawley held homemade signs in public. One of the signs said, "Tawana, We Believe You! Your Fight is our fight!"[103]

The grand jury that investigated the Tawana Brawley case received reports from 180 witnesses, reviewed 250 exhibits, and recorded more than 6,000 pages of testimony. She was found in a trash bag on November 28, 1987, and on October 6, 1988 the grand jury issued a 170-page report that concluded she had not been abducted or sexually assaulted as she had claimed. Consistent with the grand jury report, an associate of Al Sharpton told the news media that Ms. Brawley's lawyers, C. Vernon Mason and Alton H. Maddox Jr., as well as Al Sharpton, were all "frauds from the beginning."[104] Apparently, Baptist minister Reverend Al Sharpton views the Ninth Commandment as nothing more than the "Ninth Suggestion!"

Al Sharpton, Tawana Brawley, and the two attorneys named above, also falsely accused Steven Pagones of being one of Tawana Brawley's rapists – even though he was an Assistant Attorney General in Dutchess County, New York. The grand jury found Sharpton guilty of making seven defamatory statements about the character of Mr. Pagones. He subsequently sued Al Sharpton and the two attorneys for defamation of character and was awarded $345.000. Sharpton never paid his share of the award, and it was eventually paid by his supporters. Steven Pagones also sued Tawana Brawley, and won his case when she failed to appear in court. She was ordered to pay him $185.000. [105] (All who are falsely accused should sue those who are clearly guilty of filing fake sex crimes and fake hate crimes allegations!)

Al Sharpton and others claimed the grand jury investigation was just a cover-up by racist whites, and to the present day Sharpton has not admitted that Ms. Brawley had perpetrated a sexual assault hoax and blamed innocent men – and nonexistent men. Despite evidence to the contrary, Ms. Brawley has also not admitted that her allegations were false. A statement provided by legal scholar Patricia J. Williams gives the reader a most fascinating peek into the leftist psyche regarding such false allegations of sexual misconduct. According to Williams, Tawana Brawley "has been the victim of some unspeakable crime. No matter how she got there. No matter who did it to her – and even if she did it to herself."[106]

The mindset of some leftists is truly frightening!

The Tawana Brawley case is just one of numerous, scandalous escapades that involved Al Sharpton, but today he is held in high regard by many members of the Left, including former President Barack Obama, MSNBC executives, various radio and television producers, and of course Hollywood moviemakers! Thus, leading a false charge of sexual misconduct against an innocent white male public official can launch an obscure individual into leftist stardom! Sadly, the Tawana Brawley escapade epitomizes the sick leftist media culture which vigorously supports Dr. Christine Blasey Ford despite the fact that there are at least 80 Reasons to disbelieve her! (For a summary of 16 very questionable escapades involving Al Sharpton, check out *NewsMax.com*.)[107]

Reason Number Seventy-Eight: Dr. Ford is a leftist feminist activist member of the Democrat Party – whose members encourage a Marxist-style victimhood mentality and generously reward "proletarians" who file false, malicious accusations against innocent "bourgeois" males who Hillary Clinton and other leftists smear as "racist, sexist, homophobic, xenophobic, Islamophobic, you name it."[108]

Like Reason Number Seventy-Seven, Reason Number Seventy-Eight does not provide evidence that Dr. Ford lied, it simply exposes a second context in which lying is generously rewarded within the corrupt leftist world in which she thrives. Like each individual reason, Reason Number Seventy-Eight must be viewed within the context of all the other reasons.

As noted in Reason Number Seventy-Seven, for years Al Sharpton has hosted his own radio program as well as a cable television show on MSNBC called *Politics Nation With Al Sharpton*. In addition, he was a frequent guest at the White House during the presidency of Barack Obama. For example, on February 27, 2015 the *DailyMail.co.uk* printed the following headline: "Home is where the POTUS is: Al Sharpton returns to White House 'for his 73RD visit' with Obama to discuss problems facing minorities."[109]

Yes, launching or supporting high-profile false allegations of misconduct against innocent people, especially innocent white, Christian males, can make you a frequent, cherished guest at the White House when a Democrat sits in the Oval Office! This topic is expanded upon in Chapter Two.

Reason Number Seventy-Nine: From early childhood through adulthood, Dr. Ford has been deeply immersed in a leftist educational system that cultivates "proletarians" and encourages a Marxist-style victimhood mentality, thereby spawning false, malicious accusations against innocent "bourgeois" males who Hillary Clinton and other leftists smear as "racist, sexist, homophobic, xenophobic, Islamophobic, you name it."[110]

Like the two previous reasons, Reason Number Seventy-Nine does not provide evidence that Dr. Ford lied, it simply exposes a third context in which lying is generously rewarded. That third context is the pervasive, leftist educational system in which she has worked both as a student and as a professor. Keep in mind that, as students, most Americans are saturated with leftist indoctrination from early childhood through early adulthood. And, the indoctrination continues for the more 3.6 million teachers[111] and 1.54 million professors[112] in America today. Like each individual reason, Reason Number Seventy-Nine must be viewed within the context of all the other reasons.

Researchers at *Econ Journal Watch* reported in their Abstract that, overall, Democrat professors outnumber Republican professors by nearly 12 to 1. In the field of History the ratio was an astounding 33.5 to 1. To no one's surprise, in the field of Journalism/Communications the ratio of Democrats to Republicans was a disappointing 20.0 to 1. In Dr. Ford's chosen field of Psychology the ratio was 17.4 to 1. In the field of Law the ratio was 8.6 to 1, and 4.5 to 1 in the field of Economics. These ratios were not based on self-reports provided the professors, but upon voter registration rolls.[113]

Equally disturbing is the report by Jenna Lawrence of *Campus-Reform.org*. Commenting on an American Enterprise Institute panel discussion titled, "The Close-Minded Campus? The Stifling of Ideas in American Universities," it was reported that "About 18 percent of social scientists in the United States self-identify as Marxists, compared to only about 5 percent who identify as conservatives, Dunn and Shields reported."[114]

(The topic of leftist indoctrination of students throughout the American educational system is covered in greater detail in Chapter Two, beginning on page 112.)

Reason Number Eighty: Lastly, Dr. Ford may be the victim of False Memory Syndrome!

As noted under Reason Number Forty-Nine: "Dr. Ford did not notify her parents nor law enforcement of the alleged assault in the 1980s. Her first report appears to be in 2012 when she spoke to her therapist."

According to Mark Moran at *Webmd.com*, "In recent years, the medical community has become increasingly aware of a phenomenon known as 'false memory syndrome,' where through therapy, people become convinced that they were sexually abused as children. In these cases — which occur mostly in women — the memories of abuse, although vivid, are false, induced by suggestion in therapy. This unfortunate, yet uncommon, side effect of therapy can tear families apart, and leave therapists confused and bewildered about what to do."[115]

In addition, at the False Memory Syndrome Foundation we find the following: "What are false memories? Because of the reconstructive nature of memory, some memories may be distorted through influences such as the incorporation of new information. There are also believed-in imaginings that are not based in historical reality; these have been called false memories, pseudo-memories, and memory illusions. They can result from the influence of external factors, such as the opinion of an authority figure or information repeated in the culture. An individual with an internal desire to please, to get better or to conform can easily be affected by such influences."[116]

Is Dr. Ford a victim of false memory syndrome? At this point in time truth-seekers may have great difficulty answering that question. We can only speculate. However, Dr. Ford apparently first raised the issue of sexual assault in therapy, and this is where false memories tend to originate and incubate. This, combined with her often confused and refuted presentation, her astounding lack of memory of numerous crucial details, and her long-term immersion in the pervasive and profusely rewarding "victim mentality" culture of the Left, leaves us with the possibility that false memory syndrome may be at play here. Again, we must view this perspective within the context of the other 79 reasons provided herein.

Given Dr. Ford's extensive background in psychology and her research into self-hypnosis, she certainly possesses the expertise necessary to plant a false memory into her own psyche!

Chapter Two

Judge Brett Kavanaugh
And The Art Of
Character Assassination!

Consensus: Character Assassination

"Let's Be Honest: The Kavanaugh Allegations Are Nothing More Than **A Political Hit Job**." – Matt Vespa, *Townhall.com*, September 24, 2018[1]

"This whole two-week effort has been a calculated and orchestrated **political hit**, fueled with apparent pent-up anger about President Trump and the 2016 election, fear that has been unfairly stoked about my judicial record, revenge on behalf of the Clintons and millions of dollars in money from outside left-wing opposition groups." – Judge Brett Kavanaugh, September 27, 2018[2]

"This is a circus. The consequences will extend long past my nomination. The consequences will be with us for decades. This grotesque and coordinated **character assassination** will dissuade competent and good people of all political persuasions from serving our country." – Judge Brett Kavanaugh, September 27, 2018[3]

"I will not be intimidated into withdrawing from this process. You have tried hard. You've given it your all. No one can question your efforts. Your coordinated and well-funded efforts to **destroy my good name** and destroy my family will not drag me out. The vile threats of violence against my family will not drive me out. You may defeat me in the final vote, but you'll never get me to quit. Never." – Judge Brett Kavanaugh, September 27, 2018[4]

"The disgust and outrage at this fiasco of **character assassination** should not be targeted at Dr. Ford. She is only a tool in this, wielded by a venal and corrupt body within the Democratic Party." – Brad Slager, *RedState.com*, September 28, 2018[5]

"But it's low and dishonorable to skip the principled opposition and simply **smear** a good man, engaging in cheap **character assassination** as Judge Kavanaugh's Democratic opponents have this week." – David French, *NationalReview.com*, September 7, 2018[6]

"This was a **lynching** of a good man for cheap political advantage and it must be punished if we are going to have less of them in the future....We defeated a calculated **smear** designed to destroy an innocent man in the name of progressive tyranny." – Kurt Schlichter, *Townhall.com*, October 11, 2018[7]

"This has all the indicators of an 11th hour **character assassination** and a desperate attempt to delay and defeat the nomination of Judge Kavanaugh, who has a sterling reputation in his community, his profession, his church, and among hundreds of friends, colleagues and co-workers." – Carrie Severino, *News-Max.com*, September 13, 2018[8]

And, "Chuck Schumer vowed to oppose Kavanaugh with everything he's got, and apparently that took the form of **character assassination**. This has all of the ingredients of a **smear campaign on steroids**." – Carrie Severino, *Confirm-Kavanaugh.com*, September, 2018[9]

"Judge Brett Kavanaugh fought off a brutal left-wing **character assassination** attempt in a Hail Mary pass to derail his nomination." – Matt Vespa, *Townhall.com*, October 9, 2018[10]

"A lot of women, including me, in America, looked up and saw a man [Judge Brett Kavanaugh] who was – is a – [victim of] political **character assassination**. And, also, we looked up and saw in him possibly our husbands, our sons, our cousins, our co-workers, our brothers." – Kellyanne Conway, Counselor to President Trump[11]

In addressing the Democrat attacks against Judge Kavanaugh, Sean Hannity stated that "every conservative" he knows has had to deal with "baseless **character smears, character assassina-tions**." He also said, "Now, the most often used **character assassination** in the Democratic playbook is to call Republicans racist." Hannity further stated that, "In fact every four years, every two years, Republicans are racist, misogynistic, homo-phobic, xenophobic, Islamophobic. Oh, they want dirty air and water, and they want to kill your children and throw granny over a cliff."[12] However, in this case they are smearing the character of a conservative named Judge Brett Kavanaugh by portraying him as a sexual miscreant.

While Watching Kavanaugh's Testimony Allie Beth Stuckey Was "Crying Like A Baby!"

Allie Beth Stuckey, a *Townhall.com* columnist who has been described by Beth Baumann as "the Conservative Millennial," posted a video on Facebook wherein she described her thoughts and feelings regarding the treatment of Judge Brett Kavanaugh by Democrats. Like Kellyanne Conway, Allie Beth Stuckey expressed sincere concern for the men in her life when she said, "I don't think I've ever felt more strongly about something that's happening politically than I do about this. I can't tell you why this is affecting me much, so deeply. I mean, I feel physi-cally ill over all of this.

"Watching his [Kavanaugh's] testimony yesterday, I was crying like a baby. I don't know if it's because I see in him every good man that I know and I just can't – I cannot fathom living in a world in which my husband or my brothers or my dad could be [charged] with something like rape and not be presumed innocent until proven guilty."

In Stuckey's heartfelt exposé she further stated that she did not wish to live in a world where people – especially men – are charged with "unsubstantiated, uncorroborated allegations" such as those presented by Dr. Ford. Moreover, such men "have the burden of proof on them," and are not perceived as innocent until proven guilty beyond a reasonable doubt. Like others, Allie Beth Stuckey described Dr. Ford as a "pawn" who has been exploited by Democrats to ruin the life of an innocent man for purely political purposes. "...**Kavanaugh's life is being ruined.** He is right. His reputation is going to be tainted forever." She noted that, just as Clarence Thomas' name is indelibly linked to that of accuser Anita Hill, Brett Kavanaugh's name will forever be associated with that of accuser Dr. Christine Blasey Ford. (Watch this captivating Facebook video at *Townhall.com*.)[13]

Allie Beth Stuckey reported accurately and with great anguish that "**Kavanaugh's life is being ruined**." She added, "And the sad part about it is you have people, so many people it seems like, on the Left who don't care, who are so bent on gaining power that they are **willing to ruin a man's life** because of it." Those statements of Allie Beth Stuckey are 100 percent correct. Ariel Dumas, a writer for "The Late Show with Stephen Colbert," posted the following on Tweeter: "Whatever happens, **I'm just glad we ruined Brett Kavanaugh's life.**"[14] The above contrasting comments represent just one glaring difference between the moral value system of a conservative woman like Allie Beth Stuckey and a leftist woman like Ariel Dumas. Why was Ariel Dumas glad that Democrats ruined the life of an innocent man?

Newt Gingrich Said The Character Assassination Of Judge Brett Kavanaugh Was "Sickening!"

As noted in Chapter One, prior to the hearings, Judge Brett Kavanaugh was personally interviewed by many senators, including Democrat Senator Diane Feinstein. Senator Feinstein received Dr. Ford's letter in July, 2018, and she interviewed Judge Kavanaugh on August 20, 2018. So, given that Senator Feinstein received the letter from Dr. Ford many weeks before she interviewed Judge Kavanaugh, why did she not question him in their private meeting about the alleged sexual assault? Why did she wait until the hearings were concluding and senators were on the verge of voting to confirm (or to not confirm) Judge Kavanaugh?

Also as noted in Chapter One, in an interview with a *Fox News* reporter, Senator Feinstein said, "I can't say everything is truthful" in Dr. Ford's letter. She later tried to "walk back" her doubts about the truthfulness of the allegation in Dr. Ford's letter. Reportedly, Dr. Ford did not want to go public with her allegation, but someone leaked the contents of the letter, and Senator Feinstein and her staff cannot be dismissed as suspects. Former Speaker of the House Republican Newt Gingrich stated on *Fox News* that Democrat Senator Feinstein "was once a responsible and honorable person," implying that she no longer demonstrates those attributes.

Senator Lindsey Graham said to his colleagues, "This is the most unethical sham since I've been in politics." He further added, "To my Republican colleagues, if you vote no [on the confirmation of Judge Kavanaugh], you're legitimizing the most despicable thing I have seen in my time in politics." Agreeing with Senator Lindsey Graham's statements, Mr. Gingrich said, "This has been the most despicable behavior, by a major party, in modern history. This is a deliberate, vicious **character assassination**."

In his continuing discussion with Laura Ingraham of *Fox News*, Mr. Gingrich further stated, "You're watching people on that panel, Democrats on that panel, who know it's a lie, they know it's a lie. They know the way Feinstein did this was utterly, totally, despicable." Mr. Gingrich further stated that this process was "sickening." He repeated that, "This is a despicable act of utter **character assassination** by people who frankly behaved in an evil way, unworthy of the United States." Mr. Gingrich pointed out that Democrats could have brought this allegation by Dr. Ford to the attention of Republicans "in the middle of the summer," but instead, "They have deliberately created a firestorm of **character assassination** at the last possible moment."[15]

Consider the following: The backbone President Trump has demonstrated in dealing with corrupt Democrats in government and in the media has become contagious – at least for some Republicans! Prior to the election of Donald Trump, Republican politicians had a long established record of folding under the slightest pressure from Democrats. Senator Lindsey Graham never exhibited the righteous indignation he displayed in exposing the flimsy, uncorroborated, and refuted allegation of Dr. Ford that Democrat Senator Diane Feinstein sprung on the Senate Judiciary Committee at the "11th hour" prior to a confirmation vote. Where did he find that courage?

President Trump Apologized To The Kavanaugh Family "On Behalf Of Our Nation" For Mistreatment By Leftists

As reported by Cortney O'Brien of *Townhall.com*, when President Trump was addressing the International Association of Chiefs of Police he spoke about the earlier confirmation hearings of Judge Kavanaugh. President Trump said he told Judge Brett Kavanaugh that his confirmation was going to be "a piece of cake." However, after the grueling confirmation hearings were over President Trump said, "The way Democrats treated him [Judge Kavanaugh] was 'disgraceful.' False statements were written about him by 'evil' people. But, we toughed it out."[16]

Gregg Re of *Fox News* noted that, at the swearing in ceremony of Judge Kavanaugh, President Trump offered the following apology: "On behalf of our nation, I want to apologize to Brett and the entire Kavanaugh family for the terrible pain and suffering you have been forced to endure. Those who step forward to serve our country deserve a fair and dignified evaluation. Not a **campaign of political and personal destruction based on lies and deception**. What happened to the Kavanaugh family violates every notion of fairness, decency and due process. In our country, a man or a woman must always be presumed innocent unless and until proven guilty."[17]

Numerous Democrats Have Assassinated The Character Of Judge Brett Kavanaugh With Zero Evidence And Zero Corroborating Witnesses

While Democrats used Dr. Christine Blasey Ford as a pawn to indirectly assassinate the character of Judge Brett Kavanaugh, many prominent Democrats assassinated his character directly. As noted in Chapter One, Democrat Senator Cory Booker stated that those who support the elevation of Judge Brett Kavanaugh to the U.S. Supreme Court are "complicit in evil," thus inferring that Judge Brett Kavanaugh is an "evil" person. Senator Richard "Stolen Valor" Blumenthal, a Democrat, said "Judge Kavanaugh is your worst nightmare."

Also as stated earlier, Democrat Senator Elizabeth "Pocahontas" Warren said Judge Brett Kavanaugh's "nomination is a threat to people of color, to women, to workers, to the LGBTQ community, to people living in poverty." Democrat Senator Kamala Harris stated that, with the nomination of Judge Kavanaugh, "We're looking at a destruction of the Constitution of the United States." Democrat Senator Jeff Merkley said, "This is a nominee who wants to pave the path to tyranny." Democrat Terry McAuliffe, the former Governor of Virginia, said, "The nomination of Judge Brett Kavanaugh will threaten the lives of millions of Americans for decades to come."[18, 19]

Via Twitter, Google design lead Dave Hogue stated that, "You are finished, @GOP. You polished the final nail for your own coffins. F**K. YOU. ALL. TO. HELL." He also wrote, "I hope the last images burned into your slimy, evil, treasonous retinas are millions of women laughing and clapping and celebrating as your souls descend into the flames." WOW! Dave Hogue smeared the character of everyone who believes in due process, the need for evidence and/or corroborating witnesses, and the presumption of innocence, characterizing them as "slimy, evil, treasonous."[20]

Why Democrats Assassinated The Character Of Judge Brett Kavanaugh

We must keep in mind that Democrats rejected Judge Brett Kavanaugh immediately after he was nominated by President Trump, and well before the hearing process began. But why? Dr. Walter E. Williams answered this question when he titled his article as follows: "It's Our Constitution – Not Kavanaugh."

According to Dr. Williams, "Those Americans rallying against Kavanaugh's confirmation are really against the U.S. Constitution rather than the man – Judge Kavanaugh – whom I believe would take seriously his oath of office to uphold and defend the Constitution."[21]

Consider the following quotes from Judge Kavanaugh:

"I do not decide cases based on personal or policy preferences. I am not a pro-plaintiff or pro-defendant judge. I am not a pro-prosecution or pro-defense judge. I am a pro-law judge."[22] And, "I revere the Constitution. I believe that an independent and impartial judiciary is essential to our constitutional republic. If confirmed by the Senate to serve on the Supreme Court, I will keep an open mind in every case and always strive to preserve the Constitution of the United States and the American rule of law."[23]

Based on Judge Kavanaugh's statements, we may conclude that he correctly believes that it is the duty of a judge to rule on the law and not fabricate law. Therefore he must be rejected by Democrats who view the U.S. Constitution and those who support it as obstacles to their "progressive" (lawless) agenda.

Many leftists agree with all of the above Democrat smears! Why? Is it because Judge Brett Kavanaugh has been subjected to a flurry of allegations of sexual misconduct by leftists who provided uncorroborated and refuted testimony – but provided no evidence and no witnesses? No, that is not why he is "evil." That's just their cover story!

Because Judge Brett Kavanaugh is viewed as a mainstream, establishment, conservative Republican, as well as a devout, practicing Catholic, they consider him to be "evil." Clearly, Judge Brett Kavanaugh fits into Hillary Clinton's "Basket of Deplorables," which she described as a massive group of people (half of Trump supporters) who are "racist, sexist, homophobic, xenophobic, Islamophobic, you name it." (As noted in Chapter One.)

The fact that Judge Kavanaugh correctly identified the United States of America as a "constitutional republic" instead of a "democracy" most certainly frightens Democrats. Why? Because in a constitutional republic the rights of a minority are protected by law and therefore a majority cannot vote to violate those rights. A lynch mob has been described as a pure form of a democracy wherein a person can be judged and punished by the majority without regard to the law or any established rules of fairness. This, of course, precisely describes the way Democrats have behaved toward Judge Brett Kavanaugh following the parade of uncorroborated, false, and ludicrous allegations launched against him.

James Madison, our fourth U.S. President and the "Father of the U.S. Constitution," stated that, "Democracies have ever been spectacles of turbulence and contention; . . . incompatible with personal security, or the rights of property; and have in general been as short in their lives, as they have been violent in their deaths."[24]

According to Plato, "And so tyranny naturally arises out of democracy, and the most aggravated form of tyranny and slavery out of the most extreme form of liberty..."[25]

Lord Acton agreed when he wrote that, "The one pervading evil of democracy is the tyranny of the majority; or rather of that party, not always the majority, that succeeds, by force or fraud, in carrying elections."[26]

In the leftist *Los Angeles Times* Marvin Simkin wrote, "Democracy is not freedom. Democracy is two wolves and a lamb voting on what to eat for lunch. Freedom comes from the recognition of certain rights which may not be taken, not even by a 99% vote."[27] And what rights may not be taken, not even by a 99% vote? Well, you can start answering that question by reviewing the rights found in the Bill of Rights! Yes, America is certainly a democracy, but it is a democracy within a constitutional republic.

Democrats, of course, refer to America as a democracy and not a constitutional republic because they seek a majority of voters who will give them a majority of senators, who in turn will give them a majority of leftist political activists on the U.S. Supreme Court who masquerade as justices. When that majority is achieved they can, for example, rob American taxpayers of their right to keep and bear arms as guaranteed by the Second Amendment – just as they have robbed American taxpayers of their right to pray, read the Bible, and post the Ten Command-ments on taxpayer-funded property – as guaranteed by the First Amendment. (See: *Misjudging Separation Of Church And State: 50 Bundled Facts You Won't Learn At Harvard Law School Or Read In The New York Times!*)

On his radio program Dennis Prager has often stated that "Truth" is not a value among the Left! For example, on January 14, 2018 he stated the following on his radio program: "The commitment to truth is zero at MSNBC." If leftists do not value truth, what do they value? According to author David Horowitz, "Power" is the greatest value among the political Left. According to David Horowitz, a former leftist radical raised by Communist parents, "When you're a radical, what you are thinking of is power. It's about power. You adopt this position, you take that reason, but it's all about power... They want to know what they can get away with...You get power and you change everything."

And what kind of change do they believe in? "These people want to destroy the system we live under... They are still seeking to overthrow the system and to create a socialist future."[28] Ultimately, closet Communists such as feminist leader Betty Friedan have been working surreptitiously "to create a Soviet America," according to David Horowitz.[29] (Betty Friedan is discussed in more detail later in this chapter.)

As Horowitz stated, "You get power and you change everything." So, leftists see the U.S. Supreme Court as the source of power that can override the President, Congress, the Constitution, and the will of the American people. That is precisely what the political Left does when it obtains power! The U.S. Supreme Court has reversed itself partially or entirely more than 200 times in the past.[30] Today, the supporters of Dr. Christine Blasey Ford do not want a U.S. Supreme Court dominated by perceived constitutionalists such as Judge Brett Kavanaugh because they fear it will reverse itself on the so-called constitutional right to an abortion (which robs the unborn of their right to life), Soviet-style separation of church and state, and other obvious fabrications invented by the political Left!

The late Phyllis Schlafly authored the book titled, *"The Supremacists: The Tyranny of Judges and How to Stop it;"* Mark R. Levin authored *"Men In Black: How The Supreme Court Is Destroying America;* and Judge Andrew P. Napolitano authored *"The Constitution in Exile: How the Federal Government has Seized Power by Rewriting the Supreme Law of the Land."* (Note: The supreme law of the land is the U.S. Constitution.) These and many other astute observers of the U.S. Supreme Court have documented the incalculable cultural destruction inflicted upon America by leftist political activists who have masqueraded as U.S. Supreme Court justices!

Democrats Destroying The Presumption Of Innocence Until Proven Guilty – But Only For Constitutionalists And Other People Who Disagree With Them!

During the confirmation process of Judge Kavanaugh, Democrat Senators Chuck Schumer and Cory Booker stated that, because Senate hearings for judicial nominees are not a trial, guilt or innocence should not influence their decision-making. And Democrat Senate Minority Leader Chuck Schumer stated flatly, "There's no presumption of innocence or guilt when you have a nominee before you."[31]

While Democrats insisted on another FBI investigation of Judge Brett Kavanaugh (his seventh), Democrat Senator Cory Booker demonstrated no interest in what the additional FBI investigation could uncover. Senator Booker stunned many by stating that it was not important to determine whether or not Judge Brett Kavanaugh was "innocent or guilty" of the serious misconduct allegations launched against him, and further stated that we should simply "move onto a new candidate." Why? Because Senator Booker stated that "enough questions have been raised." In other words, if devious people launch a full-scale smear campaign against an innocent man, that alone is enough to disqualify him from sitting on the U.S. Supreme Court. By taking such a position, Senator Cory Booker has encouraged character assassination!

In response, Donald Trump, Jr. tweeted the following: "Oh, so now that he's none of the things you **slandered him** with for weeks in order to **ruin his life** he should be out anyway whether he's guilty or not? This is not America. These people are truly sick."[32]

Hypocrites!
Democrats Do Not Practice
What They Preach!

While Senator Booker said that it was not important to determine whether or not Judge Brett Kavanaugh was "innocent or guilty" of the misconduct allegations launched against him, and further stated that we should simply "move onto a new candidate" because "enough questions have been raised," that standard was not applied to his fellow Democrats!

Only one month after destroying the reputation of Judge Brett Kavanaugh and demanding that he not be elevated to the U.S. Supreme Court because of uncorroborated and refuted allegations of sexual misconduct, four Democrats accused of sexual misconduct were elected to high office in the 2018 midterm elections! Why did they not withdraw during their campaigns, as Democrats demanded of Judge Brett Kavanaugh?

As noted by Frank Holmes of *TheHornNews.com*,[33] Democrats said we must "believe all survivors" of alleged sexual abuse – but only when the alleged abuser is a conservative! Holmes then provided four examples of Democrat politicians who were accused of sexual misconduct but were subsequently supported by fellow Democrat politicians and elected or re-elected by their Democrat constituents.

Firstly, Karen Monahan,[34] a former girlfriend of Democrat Representative Keith Ellison, claimed that she was physically and emotionally abused by this leftist politician. As evidence of his misconduct, she had a cell phone video of Representative Ellison dragging her off a bed by her feet when they lived together in 2016. He further verbally abused her with obscenities while physically abusing her.

This alleged abuse survivor also produced medical records that documented the "emotional and physical abuse from a partner" that she endured as the girlfriend of Democrat Representative Keith Ellison. In addition, several texts exchanged between Monahan and Ellison "had a nasty, threatening tone."

In spite of these allegations, in the 2018 midterm elections Democrats elected Representative Ellison to be the next Attorney General for the State of Minnesota. In other words, this alleged abuser of Karen Monahan was elected to become the top law enforcement officer for the state of Minnesota!

Secondly, a woman claimed that in 2007, when she was only 16 years old, "pro-feminist" Congressman Tony Cárdenas added a drug to the water he gave her. After she had passed out this "ultra-liberal" Democrat allegedly fondled her breasts and genitals. However, Cárdenas still received the endorsement of the Los Angeles County Democratic Party.[35] Weeks later he would win the primary with 67 percent of the vote, and go on to defeat his Republican challenger in the midterms by garnering an astounding 79 percent of the vote! So much for "progressive" Californians who claim to protect women from men such as Democrat Congressman Tony Cárdenas!

Thirdly, Senator Bob Menendez, a New Jersey Democrat, was charged with having sex with underage girls. As reported by Frank Holmes, "Federal prosecutors said they had 'specific, corroborated allegations that defendants Menendez and Melgen had sex with underage prostitutes in the Dominican Republic.'" Instead of asking Menendez to withdraw, Democrat Senator Charles Schumer of New York, who vehemently opposed the nomination of Judge Brett Kavanaugh to the U.S. Supreme Court, strongly supported this alleged Democrat child molester. Senator Schumer had his Senate Majority PAC invest $6 million into the campaign of Senator Menendez – and he was re-elected to the U.S. Senate by New Jersey voters!

Lastly, a woman named Reese Everson alleged that Representative Bobby Scott, a Virginia Democrat, punished her for refusing to be his sexual playmate. Leftist feminists claim that men in positions of power should not abuse that power by demanding sexual favors from female underlings. But this is precisely what Representative Bobby Scott's accuser alleged he did.

While serving as an intern (like Monica Lewinsky), Reese Everson said Representative Scott touched her inappropriately on two occasions and also flirted with her. When on a trip to California,

Scott told Everson she should not "be good" if she wanted to advance. When she refused to submit to his overtures, Scott fired her.

As reported by Adam Edelman of *NBCnews.com*,[36] Reese Everson said "I was prevented from moving forward in my career because I attempted to run from a situation that was sexually inappropriate, where I had been propositioned to have a sexual relationship with my boss that I did not want."

While Democrats say every woman must be believed, the allegation of Reese Everson was dismissed and Bobby Scott was not asked to withdraw. Instead, in the 2018 midterm elections he was re-elected and may become the Chairman of the House Education and Labor Committee!

According to Democrats, the accusations of misconduct lodged by Dr. Christine Blasey Ford, Julie Swetnick, and Deborah Ramirez must be taken seriously, but the allegations of misconduct made by Karen Monahan, Reese Everson, and others (such as Bill Clinton's accuser, Juanita Broaddrick) must be dismissed! How hypocritical!

When these four Democrats were campaigning for high office, where were the leftist feminists who demonstrated around the country against the presidential campaign of "womanizer" Donald Trump in 2016 and the nomination of Judge Brett Kavanaugh in 2018? Like sexual predators Bill Clinton and Ted Kennedy, these four Democrats also received the support of leftist feminists. Don't they know, or care, that millions of informed Americans can see their shameful, blatant hypocrisy? They know, but they simply don't care – as long as they win and seize power over their prey! Clearly, Democrats are defenders of women in their public lives, and abusers of women in their private lives!

Democrat Feminists
Chastised Republican White Women
For Not Voting For Democrat Politicians!

Three hard-left politicians, Beto O'Rourke of Texas, Stacey Abrams of Georgia, and Andrew Gillum of Florida, lost their races during the 2018 midterm elections. How did leftist feminists rationalize these losses? They blamed white women. While black women voted almost unanimously for O'Rourke (95%) and Abrams (97%), and 82 percent supported Gillum, most white women voted for their Republican opponents: Ted Cruz (59%), Brian Kemp (76%) and Ron DeSantis (51%), respectively.[37]

A tweet by the leftist Women's March stated that, "There needs to be accountability and an honest reckoning. There's a lot of work to do, white women. A lot of learning. A lot of growing."

Jill Filipovic tweed the following: "I'll be honest that the DeSantis numbers don't surprise me. White women have long voted Republican, but have been (slowly) moving Dem, and educated white women are strong Dems. Trump had less support from white women than Romney, etc. But 76% for Kemp... racism is a helluva drug."

This is an illogical conclusion since white women split their vote while black women voted nearly 100% for Stacy Abrams, who is a black woman.

Jemele Hill,[38] a staff writer for *The Atlantic* tweeted, "It's not just Texas when 53 percent of white women voted for Donald Trump. The data shows very clearly that there are white women voting against their own best interests to preserve a patriarchy that they believe will ultimately help them. Not all, but clearly the majority." Hill further tweeted, "I'm not here to antagonize white women at all. I just want to know why so many of them seem intent on voting against the best interest of all women. They need to be held accountable, particularly as in race after race, black women show up and vote in support of feminist ideals."

A short but powerful response to the tweets produced by these leftist feminists came from conservative actress Patricia Heaton: "I know this is hard for you to grasp, but women of all kinds who are pro-science and anti-violence don't believe that ending the life of your developing son or daughter in your womb is liberating or progressive. It's tyrannical and barbaric."[39]

Conservative Allie Beth Stuckey, who "cried like a baby" while watching Judge Brett Kavanaugh defend his character against leftist character assassins, wrote the following: "The claim is that we are voting against our own interests. But this assumes our interests are liberal interests – abortion, closing the 'gender pay gap,' gun control, etc. And they're just not. We women who vote Republican do so because, in general, we believe in things like the Second Amendment, lower taxes and restrictions on killing the unborn." She added, "We are not oppressed. We're just not progressive."[40]

Allie Beth Stuckey further noted that leftist feminists "completely ignore successful conservative women" such as former South Carolina Governor and U.S. Ambassador to the UN, Nikki Haley (who is an Indian-American), former U.S. Secretary of State Condoleezza Rice (who is black), and Carly Fiorina, a former CEO of Hewlett Packard and presidential candidate.

Stuckey also reminded leftist feminist that Republican women who ran in the 2018 midterm elections, such as Martha McSally, a veteran U.S. Air Force fighter pilot; Kay Ivey, the first female

Governor of Alabama; and Young Kim, the first Korean-American elected to Congress, do not fit the leftist feminist stereotype of conservative women who submit to an American patriarchy!

Allie Beth Stuckey also noted that leftist feminists "deemed women who supported Kavanaugh 'gender traitors.'" She concluded that, "Progressive feminists fancy themselves rebellious disruptors, but it's a fantasy. They're mainstream, their platform is tired, their hypocrisy is predictable and their constant bullying of women on the other side of the aisle is nauseatingly unattractive."

Perhaps at this point it should be noted that, as of January, 2019, more than 60 million abortions have been performed in the United States. Therefore, thanks to leftist feminists who claim to be defenders of women and children, at least 30 million unborn females have lost their lives to date in America through abortion! Clearly, it is the pro-life conservative women who vote in the "best interest" of all females – because, unlike left-wing women, right-wing women do not lethally discriminate against the most vulnerable females among us – the unborn!

A Few Examples Of Democrat Media Character Assassination

CNN Falsely Injects Race Into Trump Quotes

On CNN, which President Trump often criticizes for frequently spewing "fake news," Ana Cabrera spoke about President Trump and Donald Trump, Jr. and their reactions regarding the treatment of Judge Brett Kavanaugh. However, instead of accurately reporting what President Trump and Donald Trump, Jr. actually said, Cabrera claimed the following: "President Trump and his son Don Jr. said this week white men have a lot to fear right now."[41]

As stated elsewhere, President Trump actually said, "It's a very scary time for young men in America, where you can be guilty of something that you may not be guilty of." Donald Trump, Jr. simply said he was concerned more for his sons than his daughters due to the fear of false allegations. Neither President Trump nor his son mentioned race, yet this CNN pundit falsely injected race into their statements. No wonder CNN's ratings are in the dumper!

At this point ask yourself these questions: Why are Democrats frequently bashing and smearing white people, both male and female? Why do Democrats often introduce race into a discussion when race is not relevant to the topic at hand? Why do Democrats falsely accuse Republicans of racism and falsely accuse them of making racist statements? Study Marxism and its relentless call for proletariat/bourgeoisie programmed conflict and the answers to these questions become obvious!

CNN Downplays Refutations By Mark Judge And Patrick J. Smyth That Supported Judge Kavanaugh

Rich Noyes of *NewsBusters.com* headlined an article as follows: "CNN Gives Virtually No Air Time to Pro-Kavanaugh Evidence." Noyes pointed out that, on September 19, 2018, CNN devoted three hours and 23 minutes of airtime to the Judge Kavanaugh controversy between the hours of 4:00 am and 2:00 pm, Eastern Standard Time. A top story in the nation regarding the Judge Kavanaugh controversy was the fact that both Mark Judge and PJ (Patrick) Smyth refuted Dr. Ford's assertion that they were present when the alleged attack took place.

However, during that three hours and 23 minutes, only five minutes and eight seconds were devoted to the refutation provided by Mark Judge and a mere one minute and 23 seconds were devoted to the refutation provided by Patrick J. Smyth. One minute and 44 seconds were devoted to general references to the denials of the two men. Rich Noyes concluded that the total of eight minutes and 15 seconds of coverage given to the men's denials amounted to "a puny four percent of their total Kavanaugh coverage during the same period."[42]

NBC Smeared Kavanaugh, Hid Vital Information From The Public, Then Lied About It!

According to her attorney Michael Avenatti, Julie Swetnick reported that she attended house parties in the 1980's, and Brett Kavanaugh and his friend Mark Judge also attended. She further stated that the boys would spike punch with drugs or alcohol to make the girls easy prey. Once in this weakened condition, boys would than gang rape the girls. She stated that she was one of the many victims of the alleged gang rapes, and that she observed such behavior at many of the parties she had attended.

Of course one would ask, why didn't she report these gang rapes to authorities, and why did she continue to attend many of these parties after she had allegedly been gang raped?

Attorney Michael Avenatti informed NBC that a second girl had confirmed Julie Swetnick's allegation that a young Brett Kavanaugh, along with other boys, had spiked punch at parties and subsequently gang raped the girls who attended those parties. However, when NBC communicated with the second unnamed girl on several occasions, she denied ever witnessing any inappropriate behavior by a young Brett Kavanaugh. This second witness stated that attorney Michael Avenatti had "twisted" her words. So, what we have is another uncorrob-orated allegation against Judge Brett Kavanaugh.

While NBC eagerly reported on the allegation by Julie Swetnick, they failed to report that a second woman named as a witness by Michael Avenatti denied ever witnessing such behavior by Judge Brett Kavanaugh. It was only after he had been confirmed that NBC reported that Julie Swetnick's allegation could not be verified and that the second witness provided by Michael Avenatti said that he had "twisted" her words and she never witnessed what he had claimed.

John Nolte of *Breitbart.com* stated the following: "So what we have here is an *NBC News* eager to publish completely unfounded allegations of sexual assault against Brett Kavanaugh while at the same time hiding vitally important information that would have helped to clear Kavanaugh at the most crucial time of this scandal.

"In other words, in a partisan effort to derail Kavanaugh's confirmation, to do its part to keep Kavanaugh off the Supreme Court, *NBC News* published uncorroborated **smears** against him and then engaged in a deliberate cover up of a legitimate story that backed up Kavanaugh's claim of his innocence and his claim that there was a **coordinated campaign at work to personally destroy him.**"[43]

Kate Snow of NBC said they did not report their failure to corroborate Julie Swetnick's story and their failure to corroborate Michael Avenatti's story about a second witness until after Judge Kavanaugh had been confirmed because NBC learned of this AFTER his confirmation, and this made the story less important. However, when Senator Chuck Grassley said he wanted the FBI to investigate Michael Avenatti and Julie Swetnick, then the story became newsworthy again, and NBC thus reported it.

Kate Snow's excuse sounds credible, however, a close examination of the timeline of events and reporting exposes this as an attempt to cover-up NBC's bias (and corruption) against Judge Kavanaugh. John Sexton of *HotAir.com* closely followed the timeline of events, and he concluded that NBC learned well in advance (perhaps two days in advance) of the Kavanaugh confirmation vote that Julie Swetnick's allegation was un-confirmed and that the second witness said Michael Avenatti had "twisted" her words.

John Sexton also noted that the "less important" claim by NBC is also without merit. According to Sexton, "Frankly, the idea that this had no news value even after the vote is just nonsense. What idiot at NBC made that call? Of course, it was relevant that the accuser's lawyer seemed to be lying and meddling with statements! Is NBC not aware that a lot of Americans were furiously angry Kavanaugh had been confirmed, in part because they believed he was a gang-rapist? There was never a time when evidence that [Swetnick's and Avenatti's] story did not hold up was not worth airing."[44]

In summary, NBC aired an interview with a woman with a dubious history who made uncorroborated allegations of sexual misconduct against Judge Kavanaugh. NBC then hid crucial information from the public regarding a false witness in order to make Judge Brett Kavanaugh appear guilty of the horrendous, unsubstantiated crimes of drugging girls and engaging in serial gang rapes, then NBC lied about it when they were caught doing so. This is not journalism! This is sick. This is truly evil. This is contemporary American leftism! This is the Democrat Media Smear Machine at work in the 21st century!

In addition to hiding vital information regarding accuser Julie Swetnick, NBC also hid from their viewing audience the report issued by sex crime expert Rachel Mitchell that described Dr. Ford's allegation as weak and lacking evidence. Bill D'Agostino and Nicholas Fondacaro of *NewsBusters.com* titled their article as follows: "What Memo? NBC Ignores Prosecutor Memo Questioning Ford's Claims."[45]

NBC Presented Julie Swetnick's
Incredible Allegation As Credible
Despite Her Long, Questionable History

Based on an *Associated Press* report, Kavanaugh accuser Julie Swetnick had been involved in at least six lawsuits during the last 25 years. For example, a few weeks after Swetnick began working as a software engineer for Webtrends, an Oregon-based software company, two male co-workers complained that she displayed "unwelcome sexual innuendo and inappropriate conduct" at a business lunch. When confronted with the charges, Swetnick accused Webtrends of subjecting her to "physically and emotionally threatening and hostile conditions," and that she had been sexually harassed by four co-workers – who denied the charges. According to Webtrends, she also falsified her employment application, claiming she had earned a degree from John Hopkins University when no such degree had been earned.

In addition to the above problems, Kavanaugh accuser Julie Swetnick filed a personal injury lawsuit in Maryland against the Washington Metropolitan Area Transit Authority. According to *The Associated Press*, Swetnick claimed "she lost more than $420,000 in earnings after she hurt her nose in a fall on a train in 1992." Describing herself as a model and actor, she claimed she had "numerous modeling commitments" with several companies at the time of the accident but missed those income opportunities because of her injuries. Swetnick's lawsuit was dismissed in 1997 after a settlement was reached. However, she received no money because she could produce no documentation to support her claim that she had lost wages as a result of her injuries.[46]

NBC News seems to have been the only news organization that viewed Julie Swetnick as a credible witness even though they reported the following: "Swetnick provided *NBC News* with the names of four friends who she said went to the parties with her. One is deceased, while two others did not respond to requests for comment. A fourth told *NBC News* he didn't remember Swetnick." Recall that Dr. Ford claimed four others were at the party where she was allegedly assaulted, but none could verify her story. Likewise, Julie Swetnick produced the names of four people who she claimed could verify her story, but none did![47]

So, NBC went so far as to interview Julie Swetnick even though her allegation was absurd on its face, stating that Brett Kavanaugh and Mark Judge drugged girls at parties so the girls could be gang raped. And she said she was gang raped at one of the parties, but did not report it to the police, and she repeatedly attended parties where gang rapes were occurring. John Nolte of *Breitbart.com* titled one of his articles as follows: "Nolte: 28 Reasons Julie Swetnick's Kavanaugh Allegations Are Total Garbage."[48] However, despite the ludicrous allegations made by Julie Swetnick, like other leftist political activists, *NBC News* used her as a pawn to assassinate the character of Judge Kavanaugh.

That is why *NBC News* gave Julie Swetnick an exclusive televised interview knowing her allegation was absurd on its face, knowing her record of numerous lawsuits and falsifying an employment application, knowing they could not verify her story because none of the witnesses she named confirmed that she even attended such parties, and knowing that *The New York Times* and other leftist news organizations passed on this exceedingly flimsy story. Clearly, *NBC News* is not simply biased, *NBC News* is corrupt!

Matt Vespa of *Townhall.com* stated the following regarding the allegations made by Deborah Ramirez, Julie Swetnick, and Dr.

Christine Blasey Ford: "Deborah Ramirez and Julie Swetnick also came forward, with Swetnick's being the most ludicrous. She alleged that Kavanaugh was part of a gang rape ring in high school. Ramirez alleges Kavanaugh exposed himself at a party at Yale. *The New York Times* didn't even run stories on both these women because they couldn't confirm anything. And *The New Yorker*, who first detailed the Ramirez allegation, couldn't do either in a follow up piece by Ronan Farrow and Jane Mayer. All three accusations were without witnesses or evidence. And the timing made things look even more suspect."[49]

The key sentences here are the following: "All three accusations were without witnesses or evidence. And the timing made things look even more suspect."

Yes, "the timing made things look even more suspect" because all the allegations were presented to Senator Chuck Grassley, the Chairman of the Judiciary Committee, AFTER senators had finished personally interviewing Judge Kavanaugh in individual sessions; AFTER senators had finished their questioning of Judge Kavanaugh in open hearings, and AFTER it appeared Judge Kavanaugh would be confirmed to sit on the U.S. Supreme Court because nothing could be found to disqualify him – even after six FBI investigations into his private and professional life.

Senator Lindsey Graham Labels NBC A "Co-Conspirator" In The Character Assassination Of Judge Brett Kavanaugh

Senator Lindsey Graham provided the following criticism of NBC for airing as a legitimate news story the contents of an anonymous letter with no return address: "Well NBC, here's the biggest offense to me, they've been a **co-conspirator in the destruction of Kavanaugh** from my point of view. There was an anonymous letter received by Cory Gardner, the Senator from Colorado with no return address, no information, just a letter, accusing Brett Kavanaugh of assaulting somebody in a restaurant in 1998 in Colorado. Cory hands it to the committee and somebody on the Democratic side leaked that letter, it got on the *NBC Nightly News*. The fourth allegation!" Senator Graham added: "Do you think NBC would have done that if it was a Democratic male nominee? All I can say is that the journalists' integrity has been destroyed over this case."[50, 51]

A Few Good Headlines
Highlighting Democrat Media Corruption

Below are a few headlines from *NewsBusters.com* and other news sources that demonstrate the corruption within the leftist news media regarding President Donald Trump – the man who nominated Judge Kavanaugh for the U.S. Supreme Court:

TV News Buries Trump's Defeat of ISIS in Iraq and Syria – Bill D'Agostino, *NewsBusters.com*, October 23, 2018.[52]

How much does CNN hate Trump? 93% of coverage is negative – Joseph Curl, *WashingtonTimes.com*, May 23, 2017.[53]

NYT Defends Publishing Short Story Imagining Assassination of Trump – Melanie Arter, *CNSnews.com*, October 26, 2018.[54]

AP Falsely Reports Trump is Kicking Immigrants Out Of The Military – Brian McNicoll, *AIM.org*, July 9, 2018.[55]

5 Biggest Media LIES about Trump...This Month! – Frank Holmes, *TheHornNews.com*, December 26, 2017.[56]

96 Percent of Google Search Results on Trump Slant Left – Kaylee McGhee, *LibertyHeadlines.com*, August 28, 2018.[57]

Study: Economic Boom Largely Ignored as TV's Trump Coverage Hits 92% Negative – Rich Noyes, *NewsBusters.com*, October 9, 2018.[58]

Within the article with the above headline, Rich Noyes noted that, of the ABC, CBS and NBC evening news coverage from June 1, through September 30, 2018, **82 percent of the reporting on Trump's nomination of Judge Brett Kavanaugh was negative**; 90 percent of the reporting on Trump's handling of North Korea was negative; 94 percent was negative regarding President Trump's handling of immigration; 97 percent of the reporting regarding the alleged Russian "collusion" investigation was negative; and an astounding 99 percent of the reporting on Trump's relation with Putin was negative.

WOW! That's not bias – that's corruption! That's not news reporting – that's Manchurian-style propaganda! Also consider the below two headlines and the following Mark Levin quote (The below material is repeated from pages 51 and 52):

Broadcasters grant only 4% of Brett Kavanaugh news coverage to judge's side of story: Study. – Jennifer Harper, *Washington-Times.com*, September 26, 2018.[59]

Nolte: *NBC News* Hid Information that Would Have Cleared Kavanaugh of Avenatti Rape Allegations – John Nolte, *Breitbart.com*, October 26, 2018.[60]

"The Media Research Center says that 90 percent of the news coverage has been negative toward Kavanaugh. Honestly, I'm surprised it's that low. It looks like 99.9 percent to me." – Mark Levin, *Life, Liberty & Levin,* October 7, 2018[61]

Democrat Media Corruption
Overshadows Their Bias

Leftist so-called journalists and reporters do not show occasional favoritism or intermittent infatuation, as one would expect if they were simply biased. Instead, they consistently engage in "Manchurian-style" psychological manipulation of the masses. They routinely provide protection for politicians who advocate leftist principles and practices and they launch savage, merciless, venomous attacks against those who oppose them. That is not the kind of behavior one would expect from people who are simply biased. However, that is precisely the kind of behavior one would expect from people who are corrupt. That is precisely the kind of behavior one would expect from morally-challenged individuals who are pushing a leftist political agenda while masquerading as objective journalists and reporters.

Note the difference in media coverage of President Barack Obama when compared to that of President Donald Trump:

Back in 2011, Brian Montololi of *CBSnews.com* reported the following: "President Obama 'has suffered the most unrelentingly negative treatment' of all presidential candidates over the past five months, according to a study released Monday from the Pew Research Center's Project for Excellence in Journalism.

"Pew found that Mr. Obama was the subject of negative assessments nearly four times as often as he was the subject of positive assessments. It found he received 'positive' coverage nine percent of the time, 'neutral' coverage 57 percent of the time and 'negative' coverage 34 percent of the time."[62]

So, three years into his presidency Barack Obama "suffered the most unrelenting negative treatment" and endured "harsh media coverage" with negative news "coverage at 34 percent."

Two years into his presidency Donald Trump has had to endure 92 percent negative news coverage. If Obama "suffered" and endured "harsh media coverage" with negative news coverage at 34 percent, what does Trump endure with negative news coverage at 92 percent?

Is Dr. Christine Blasey Ford A Virtual Manchurian Candidate?

"In today's world, you no longer need bullets to assassinate leaders." – Matt Vespa, *Townhall.com*, September 24, 2018.[63]

The 1959 novel, *The Manchurian Candidate*, was authored by Richard Condon. His book was adapted into a movie in 1962 and again in 2004. In this political thriller an American soldier is captured during the Korean War and taken to Manchuria, which is a large area within Northeast Asia. As a POW the American soldier is brainwashed by Communist Chinese and Soviet intelligence officers. After returning home to America he works unwittingly as a political assassin for Communist forces.

Today, loosely, a Manchurian Candidate may be defined as someone who has been brainwashed or programmed to perform specific activities, most notably assassination – thus causing the death of one or more targeted individuals, especially for political purposes. The Manchurian Candidate is activated by a specific code provided by a handler, and the assassin has no knowledge of being brainwashed and no memory of engaging in homicide – whether it was performed literally or metaphorically. When questioned about an assassination, the Manchurian Candidate is unable to answer basic, fundamental questions regarding the event.

While examining the behavior of Dr. Christine Blasey Ford as displayed on television and recorded in numerous articles, the concept of Manchurian Candidate came to mind. While Dr. Ford is not a textbook Manchurian Candidate, she may be described as a "Virtual Manchurian Candidate." Many of her behaviors are truly inexplicable. Over a period of several weeks Dr. Ford had displayed profound memory loss for both past and recent events, and had displayed sloppy thinking while launching serious accusations which have been uncorroborated or refuted by four people she had named as witnesses.

As noted elsewhere in this book, for a woman who has a Ph.D. and functions as a professor of psychology at Palo Alto University and a research psychologist at the Stanford University School of medicine, this is very incongruent and disturbing behavior. How could she be so intellectually incompetent as an accuser, but function at a high level of intellectual competence as a professor and a researcher?

How can this incongruent behavior be explained? Is she a liar? Would she knowingly and repeatedly commit perjury while under oath? If so, perhaps she may be a "Virtual Manchurian Candidate." That is, she may be a woman who has been programmed at various levels in the leftist education establishment and by the leftist media to be a "no-holds barred," warrior feminist. Moreover, she may consider such programming to be normal, or even necessary, and has therefore eagerly embraced it. If so, she has embraced the programming that has prepared her to assassinate the character of constitutionalists, or a specific constitutionalist, who may be nominated to the U.S. Supreme Court!

For many weeks Dr. Ford behaved like a high-tech, Virtual Manchurian Candidate programmed to assassinate not the body, but the character, of Judge Brett Kavanaugh! Those who consider Dr. Ford to be a pawn may be correct, but she may be a pawn in a way that few people may suspect!

When Associate Justice Clarence Thomas defended himself against allegations of sexual misconduct during his 1991 senate hearings, he told his critics that he was being subjected to a "high-tech lynching." In other words, he was not being physically lynched, as Democrats often did to blacks in the Deep South, but rather it was a "high-tech lynching" in that his character was being assassinated via television, radio, and the modern printing press. Likewise, Brett Kavanaugh was not being physically assassinated by Democrats (although some leftists have threatened his life), but rather his character was being assassinated by the same "high-tech" political machine that assassinated the character of Justice Clarence Thomas — not to mention the character of Judge Robert Bork!

Below are quotes from Clarence Thomas' October 11, 1991 Senate Judiciary Committee hearing after Anita Hill launched charges of sexual misconduct against him while he was being considered for a seat on the U.S. Supreme Court:

"I think that this today is a travesty. I think that it is disgusting. I think that this hearing should never occur in America. This is a case in which this sleaze, this dirt, was searched for by staffers of members of this committee, was then leaked to the media, and this committee and this body validated it and displayed it at prime time over our entire nation.

"This is not an opportunity to talk about difficult matters privately or in a closed environment. This is a circus. It's a national disgrace. And from my standpoint as a black American, as far as I'm concerned, it is a **high-tech lynching** for uppity blacks who, in any way, deign to think for themselves, to do for themselves, to have different ideas, and it is a message that unless you kowtow to an old order, this is what will happen to you. You will be lynched, destroyed, caricatured by a committee of the U.S. – U.S. Senate, rather than hung from a tree."[64, 65]

In other words, Clarence Thomas was charging leftist Democrat senators with conducting a virtual lynching, which he described as a "high-tech lynching." Thus, we may view a "Virtual Manchurian Candidate" as synonymous with a "High-tech Manchurian Candidate" who destroys the character of individuals such as Justice Clarence Thomas, Judge Robert Bork, and Judge Brett Kavanaugh.

Dictionary.com defines the word "virtual" as follows:

Adjective

1.   being such in power, force, or effect, though not actually or expressly such:

       a virtual dependence on charity.

2.   Optics.

a.   noting an image formed by the apparent convergence of rays geometrically, but not actually, prolonged, as the image formed by a mirror (opposed to real).

b.   noting a focus of a system forming virtual images.

3.   temporarily simulated or extended by computer software:

       a virtual disk in RAM; virtual memory on a hard disk.

Note the definition of "virtual" contains the words "simulated," "not actually," and is something that is "opposed to real," and therefore not actually real while appearing so.

Therefore, a Real Manchurian Candidate would be programmed to assassinate the body of targeted individuals for political purposes. Contrastingly, a Virtual Manchurian Candidate, as defined here, would be programmed to assassinate the character of targeted individuals for political purposes. The Virtual Manchurian Candidate is "not actually" a genuine assassin, but someone who simulates an assassin by killing the reputation and destroying the career of targeted individuals. As stated above by Matt Vespa of *Townhall.com*, "In today's world, you no longer need bullets to assassinate leaders."

While Democrats Said
Dr. Ford Had Nothing To Gain,
Dr. Ford Said Thanks For The Money

Among the more than 20 million viewers who watched the September 27, 2018 Senate Judiciary Committee testimony of Dr. Christine Blasey Ford, some may recall the following statements:

"You had absolutely nothing to gain by bringing these facts to the Senate Judiciary Committee." – Democrat Senator Dick Durbin

"I want to thank you because you clearly have nothing to gain for what you have done." – Democrat Senator Kamala Harris

However, as reported by Paul Sperry of *RealClearInvestigations.com*,[66] Dr. Christine Blasey Ford had a shocking amount to gain. Firstly, she was flooded with generous donations. At the time of this writing the *GoFundMe.com* account set up under the title "Help Christine Blasey Ford" received $645,707 in donations. The account titled, "To Cover Dr. Ford's Security Costs," had raised $209,982. Lastly, the "Honor Dr. Blasey As An Educator" account garnered $32,420 in donations. This last account was set up "To honor her, particularly in her professional capacity, this is a campaign to raise funds to endow an academic chair (professorship) and/or scholarships, to be named so as to recognize Dr. Blasey."

The question being asked is, why does she need all this money? For starters we know that her attorneys, who are fellow leftist political activists, were working pro bono, so she had no attorney fees to pay. In addition, her Democrat attorneys paid for her polygraph testing. Also, Democrats were allotted a half-million dollars to cover the costs of her transportation, security, and associated investigations. It was also noted that "The Senate Sergeant at Arms and Capitol Police also provided 'heightened security' for Ford."

Dr. Ford stated that she had to procure 24/7 security protection due to numerous threats, and she had moved at least four times. However, it had been noted that she and her family have stayed at the home of relatives, and they also relocated to their beach house in Santa Cruz, California. So it appears she was not paying high fees for hotels or other expensive accommodations.

Moreover, the Ford family is financially quite comfortable, even without the *GoFundMe.com* accounts. For example, both Dr. Ford and her husband have well-paying jobs. The home they own in Palo Alto is valued at $3.3 million, and their beach house has an estimated market value of $1.03 million. A decade ago they sold a Bed & Breakfast for more than $1.5 million. However, she had encouraged people to continue donating to the *GoFundMe.com* accounts that had been set up to help defray the expenses associated with her testimony against Judge Brett Kavanaugh.

On November 27, 2018, Danielle Garrand at *MSN.com* stated that, "Ford wrote she has closed the GoFundMe account for further contributions. All unused donations 'after completion of security expenditures will be donated to organizations that support trauma survivors,' she wrote. Ford said she is currently researching organizations to direct the leftover funds and will use the GoFundMe to provide an update later on."[67]

According to Paul Sperry of *RealClearInvesitgations.com*,[68] "Some legal analysts worry her [Dr. Ford's] crowdfunding windfall sets a dangerous precedent by creating a new incentive for accusers. They fear partisan activists will now offer crowdfunding as a form of bounty on political foes, or to buy witness testimony against political adversaries."

Jonathan Turley, a George Washington University Law School professor and *Fox News* legal analyst said, "You could have people effectively in a market for witnesses. You could buy a witness, effectively, by funding them as long as they're saying the things you want them to say."[69]

Justice Kavanaugh Said
I Don't Want The Money

Contrastingly, on October 6, 2018, the day Judge Kavanaugh became Justice Kavanaugh, a *GoFundMe.com* account set up by a conservative blogger had collected $611,645 on his behalf. However, while Dr. Ford encouraged donations and thanked those who contributed, Justice Kavanaugh declined to accept any money. His legal team provided the following response:

"Justice Kavanaugh did not authorize the use of his name to raise funds in connection with the GoFundMe campaign. He was not able to do so for judicial ethics reasons. Judicial ethics rules caution judges against permitting the use of the prestige of judicial office for fundraising purposes. Justice Kavanaugh will not accept any proceeds from the campaign, nor will he direct that any proceeds from the campaign be provided to any third party. Although he appreciates the sentiment, Justice Kavanaugh requests that you discontinue the use of his name for any fundraising purpose."

Due to Justice Kavanaugh's response, those who had donated were given the opportunity to receive a refund. At the time of this writing, the *GoFundMe.com* account had decreased to $490,296. Because Judge Kavanaugh had coached girls' basketball for the Catholic Youth Organization (CYO), the remaining funds would be donated equally among the CYO, the Tuition Assistance Fund, and the Victory Youth Center, all of which fall under the jurisdiction of the Archdiocese of Washington.

Justice Brett Kavanaugh's refusal to accept any funds is made more impressive in light of the fact that the leftist *Yahoo! News Reports* stated the following: "Supreme Court justices are actually not bound by the codified ethics rules that apply to other federal judges, the Code of Conduct for United States Judges."[70] If this is correct, like Dr. Ford, Justice Kavanaugh could have encouraged people to donate to the *GoFundMe.com* account set up for him, and he could have used those funds for personal benefit, but he chose to adhere to the standards set up for other U.S. judges. What does all this say about the character of the two individuals who are the focus of this book?

Dr. Ford Gains Fame As Well As Fortune!

In addition to the enormous financial benefit that Dr. Ford has enjoyed as a result of her public allegation against Judge Brett Kavanaugh, she will be forever immortalized by leftist political activists – despite the fact that she has been thoroughly discredited!

As a revered heroine of the political Left, Dr. Christine Blasey Ford experienced immediate benefits, and will enjoy long-term personal and professional benefits as well as the financial benefits already discussed!

Dr. Christine Blasey Ford is a leftist feminist activist, just as Barack Obama was a leftist community organizer activist, and before launching her attack against the character of Judge Brett Kavanaugh, she knew in advance that she would receive favorable coverage from the dominant leftist news media – and Judge Kavanaugh would be portrayed as a villain – much like President Trump – the man who nominated him!

As noted by Paul Sperry,[71] "Local media reported that demonstrators also gathered around her home, almost all of whom were sympathetic neighbors, friends and other supporters, not protesters. Dozens of supporters last month lined her street and interlinked arms to form a human wall in front of her house to 'protect Christine.' A few days later another 2,000 people turned out for a candlelight vigil to support Ford in her largely liberal neighborhood."

Aris Folley of *TheHill.com* noted that "Women across the globe are sending postcards in a show of support to Christine Blasey Ford, the college professor who accused Supreme Court Justice Brett Kavanaugh of sexual assault while they were in high school.

"BBC reported on Wednesday that women from the United States, Canada, Germany, the United Kingdom, and even Australia have been mailing cards to Ford's publicly-available work address, as she has reportedly been unable to return to her home due to 'unending' death threats."[72]

As reported by Nicholas Hautman of *USmagazine.com*, Dr. Ford received glowing support from many celebrities. For example, actress and leftist political activist Alyssa Milano attended the hearing as a guest of Democrat Senator Diane Feinstein. She tweeted, "I believe Dr. Christine Blasey Ford." Television talk show host Ellen DeGeneres tweeted, "Dr. Ford, I am in awe of your bravery." Showing solidarity, actress Ashley Judd tweeted, "I do not know how I got home after I was raped at 15. No memory of it. Neither does she." Actress Mia Farrow tweeted, "Deepest gratitude to you #DrChristineBlaseyFord. You told us that you are 'terrified' – but today you embody courage."[73]

In addition to the above celebrity tweets, Michael Avenatti, the attorney who represented Julie Swetnick despite her ludicrous allegations of sexual misconduct against Judge Brett Kavanaugh, embarrassed himself by sending the following tweet: "I have witnessed well over 500 witnesses testify in court and in deposition over the course of my career. There is no question that Dr. Ford is credible. This nomination must be withdrawn immediately and an honest, moral individual should be nominated. America deserves better."[74]

As noted in Chapter One, to show their solidarity with accuser Anita Hill, in 1991 a full-page advertisement in *The New York Times* contained the names of 1,600 black female supporters. In September, 2018, 1,600 fact-phobic males took out a similar full-page ad in the same newspaper with a banner message that said, "We believe Anita Hill. We also believe Christine Blasey Ford."[75] More than 600 women who graduated from Yale University since 1966 signed a letter in support of alumnus accuser Deborah Ramirez, and the signers extended their support to Dr. Christine Blasey Ford.[76] And, at the time of this writing, 1,234 women who graduated from Holton-Arms, the high school from which Dr. Ford had graduated, signed an open letter claiming their support for Dr. Ford.[77] This, however, represents only a partial list of the widespread public support Dr. Ford received from admirers from not only across America, but from around the world!

Three months after giving her testimony to the Senate Judiciary Committee, *Sports Illustrated* magazine produced a video with Dr. Ford as the presenter of the Sports Illustrated Inspiration of the Year Award to Rachel Denhollander. This, of course, was just another attack against the character of Justice Brett Kavanaugh.

Why? As noted by Katie Pavlich, Rachel Denhollander was a bona fide victim of sexual abuse by Larry Nassar, a man who may have sexually abused more than 300 women. Katie Pavlich noted that, "It is quite a shame *Sports Illustrated* chose Ford, who has been thoroughly discredited, to give this award. Their choice diminishes Denhollander's experience and the experiences of the other sexual assault victims." She concluded by stating that, "Ford is no Rachael Denhollander and Kavanaugh is no Larry Nassar. The implication there are any similarities is **another disgusting smear**" against Justice Kavanaugh.[78]

U.S. Schools, Colleges & Universities Are Virtual Manchurian Candidate Factories

Thou Shalt Bear False Witness Against Thy Neighbour!

There may be millions of Dr. Christine Blasey Ford-like Virtual Manchurian Candidates throughout America. According the Dr. Thomas Sowell, the brainwashing begins in elementary school.

Dr. Thomas Sowell, a senior fellow at the Hoover Institution at Stanford University, has investigated the widespread application of brainwashing techniques. The results of his investigation were reported in his 1993 book titled, *Inside American Education: The*

Decline, The Deception, The Dogmas. Dr. Sowell reported that the brainwashing techniques he investigated were developed in totalitarian countries, with some techniques having their roots in Communist China (which includes Manchuria) under Mao Zedong. Chairman Mao, the Communist who established communism in the nation of China, may be the deadliest genocidal maniac in human history, with a body count exceeding 76 million men, women, and children.[79] This mind-boggling body count does not include the Chinese victims of abortion – which alone may exceed 400 million.[80, 81] The Communist Chinese abortion body count is much higher than the total number of people living in the United States and Canada combined in 2019!

According to Dr. Thomas Sowell the brainwashing techniques developed under Mao and other totalitarian dictators were in widespread use in the 1990s in American public elementary and secondary schools when he conducted his research. Therefore we may ask, was Dr. Christine Blasey Ford (and her like-minded supporters, handlers, and fellow accusers) subjected to these Communist Chinese/Manchurian-style brainwashing techniques when she attended leftist elementary and secondary schools in America? Is this brainwashing continuing in the 21st century?

When researching the application of "values clarification" in America's public schools, I turned to the Index of *Inside American Education: The Decline, The Deception, The Dogmas*. Under the topic of "values clarification" I was stunned to find the following parenthetical words: (see Brainwashing). Perhaps even more surprisingly, under "Brainwashing" there were 24 separate topics wherein brainwashing in American schools was discussed, with "values clarification" being just one of those 24 topics.[82]

In discussing his book titled *The Professors: The 101 Most Dangerous Academics in America*, David Horowitz characterized the form of feminism taught in American colleges and universities today by stating that, "It's a Marxist form of feminism."[83] Therefore males, especially conservative Christian white males such as Brett Kavanaugh, are viewed as members of the bourgeoisie (those with traditional middle class values) – which are the enemy that must be destroyed by the proletariat, including the feminist proletariat!

David Horowitz also authored *One Party Classroom: How Radical Professors at America's Top Colleges Indoctrinate Students and Undermine Our Democracy.*[84] These books expose the sinister type of educational indoctrination that women like Dr. Christine Blasey Ford were immersed in as college students. (The brain-washing that occurs throughout the American educational system is explored in detail in Chapter 5 of the book, *Welcome to Soviet America: Special Edition*.)

In a must-see *Youtube.com* video titled, *To Understand Christine Blasey Ford, Take a look at Palo Alto University*, we find that Dr. Ford is a professor at an elite private college in a community (county) that voted 73% for Hillary Clinton in 2016. Most importantly, Janice Fiamengo of the University of Ottawa tells us that, "In Blasey Ford's world there can be nothing more heroic than what she is doing, and she will be applauded and rewarded for the rest of her life."[85] Why, because Palo Alto University "promotes leftist social justice activism...to an extraordinary degree." Palo Alto University actually offers a Bachelor of Science degree in Psychology and Social Action.

To the dismay of those who believe the purpose of a university is to educate students, "social justice" is ranked as the highest "core value" at Palo Alto University, while "High quality scientific research and scholarship" is ranked third. At this elite private university, female professors make up 66.7 percent of the faculty and female students make up 79 percent of the student body. Male students are treated as second class citizens; many

114

programs are designed specifically for women, but none are designed specifically for men.

"In her safe environment [on the Palo Alto University campus], Christine Blasey Ford will almost never have to encounter a view contrary to that **female victim glorifying culture** that has been fostered over decades by feminist activists. According to the feminist paradigm, Ford has reached the pinnacle of achievement: **smearing** a powerful conservative man with nothing more than her trembling voice."[86]

Yes, David Horowitz is correct, what is taught in colleges and universities today is a Marxist form of feminism, with Dr. Ford playing her role as a brave proletarian who is challenging – and destroying the character of – a member of the bourgeoisie!

In *Welcome to Soviet America: Special Edition* (Page 311), we find the following: "Keep in mind that the Soviet American Cultural Revolution began in the mid 1960s, and that the modern women's liberation movement began in 1963 with the publication of Betty Friedan's book, *The Feminine Mystique*. David Horowitz, who abandoned his Marxist roots and switched sides to become a courageous conservative American culture warrior, has investigated Betty Friedan and her politics. Horowitz points out that while she presented herself to the public as a middle class (bourgeois) woman who felt trapped in her role as a traditional American housewife, Betty Friedan was actually a closet Communist. She was striving to liberate women, but she did not seek an American form of liberation. Instead, as a Communist, her job was to create a feminist proletariat. Her job was to liberate women from their roles as transmitters of traditional American values and transform them into transmitters of Moscow-directed, Soviet American values. As David Horowitz wrote,[87] Betty Friedan's 'interest in women's liberation was just a subtext of her real desire to create a Soviet America.'"

In 1963 when Betty Friedan launched the feminist proletariat, to 2018 when Dr. Ford publicly accused Judge Brett Kavanaugh of sexual misconduct, we cover a period of 55 years. So, the feminist movement was launched four years before 51-year-old Christine Blasey Ford was born. Consequently, during her entire lifetime she has been thoroughly indoctrinated by the leftist-controlled education establishment and the leftist-controlled media establishment to join and support the feminist sister-hood. From childhood, to young adulthood, to middle age, she has been told that men, especially Bible-believing, Constitution-supporting, white men, are the enemy! They are not simply to be defeated, such men are to be destroyed — by any means necessary — and Bolshevik Democrats will reward you for the rest of your life for doing so!

With "social justice" indoctrination as the primary value at Palo Alto University, and "High quality scientific research and scholar-ship" ranked as a third-rate goal, we must ask, what is "social justice" as advocated by contemporary leftists? Some have simply stated that leftist "social justice" is synonymous with "political correctness," and thus synonymous with "cultural Marxism." Leftist proletarians comprise modern-day "thought police" who monitor what their neighbors do and say to be sure they do not engage in "micro-aggressions" that may offend hypersensitive leftists who have retreated into their "safe spaces" — especially on leftist campuses.

In short, contemporary leftist "social justice" warriors are Marxist-style authoritarians who punish those who disagree with them. Disagreement is labeled "hate speech," and the speaker must be punished with character assassination, physical violence, or whatever is necessary to stop or destroy them! This is the world of programmed leftist professors and programmed leftist students in countless colleges and universities across America! This is the world of Dr. Christine Blasey Ford. This is the world of those who support the public character assassination of the bourgeois judge named Brett Kavanaugh! This is why David Horowitz, Ann Coulter, and other bourgeois speakers have been physically assaulted when they invaded the intolerant "safe space" campuses of the hyper-sensitive, authoritarian, "social justice warriors," "cultural Marxists," and leftist "thought police!" (Check out the book, *The New Thought Police: Inside The Left's Assault On Free Speech And Free Minds*, by Tammy Bruce.)[88]

In 2007 Evan Coyne Maloney made a documentary film titled *Indoctrinate U*. In discussing the lack of tolerance for diversity of thought on leftist American campuses, Kevin Mooney wrote that, "Although most of America's institutions of higher learning were designed to foster debate and mold students into critical thinkers, a two-and-a-half-year investigation shows that a re-pressive political climate has taken hold in recent years – a climate where dissent is silenced and free speech is jeopar-dized." Thor Halvorssen, whose company supported the produc-tion of this documentary, stated that, "Universities have become a hostile environment for anyone interested in open discussions and critical thinking."[89]

As noted earlier, David Horowitz, perhaps more than anyone else, has studied the extent to which our colleges and univer-sities have become leftist indoctrination centers. He titled one of his books, *Indoctrination U: The Left's War Against Academic Freedom*.[90] Choosing a book title very similar to that of the above documentary film shows that Horowitz, like Maloney, has concluded that our colleges and universities have, indeed, become centers of indoctrination rather than centers of learn-ing. In order to promote diversity of thought Horowitz created the "Academic Bill of Rights" which has been passed by student governments across the USA.

David Horowitz points out that, "In a democracy, the purpose of an education is to teach students how to think, not what to think..." Unfortunately, in classrooms and lecture halls students are taught what to think, and are discouraged from learning how to think. An excerpt from Chapter Four of *Indoctrination U: The Left's War On Academic Freedom*, provided by *Encounter-Books.com* enticed the reader with the following disturbing information:

"An advanced stage of this intellectual corruption is manifest in courses and even entire departments that are devoted to indoctrination in sectarian dogmas. To take one at random, a course in 'Modern Marxist Theory,' taught by Martha Gimenez at the University of Colorado and listed in the university catalogue as Sociology 5055, describes its curriculum in this way: 'This seminar is designed to give students the ability to apply Marx's theoretical and methodological insights to the study of current topics of theoretical and political importance.' In other words, this is a course in how to be a Marxist. It is not – by its own description – an academic examination of Marxism that might also consider how Marxism has failed or why it might not provide 'insights' into current topics of importance."[91]

The leftist victim-rewarding educational system that produced, defends, and rewards Dr. Ford and her ilk, is the same corrupt system that produced her political activist attorneys. It is the same corrupt system that manufactured the fact-phobic politicians, professors and students who support Dr. Ford's claimed victimhood. It is the same corrupt system that produced the pro-Ford/anti-Kavanaugh/anti-Trump members of the devious leftist news media. They all want to be proletarian victims or defenders of those victims against an "oppressive" bourgeoisie – those with the traditional American, middle class values of Judge Brett Kavanaugh!

Of course, victims need a strong champion to defend them, whether those victims are women, blacks, Hispanics, children, spotted owls, or the climate. By generating an endless parade of victims, Bolshevik Big Brother Democrats can justify the creation of their massive, expensive, all-seeing, all-powerful, Soviet-style government bureaucracies designed to monitor proletariat/ bourgeoisie interactions in order to "protect" those hapless "victims" from their evil oppressors – whether those victims are real or fabricated! This, of course, is classical Marxism!

Leftist Students & Professors: "I Wanna Be A Victim, Too!"

In an article titled, "Made-Up Hate Crimes Out of Control as Victimhood Is Extolled on College Campuses," we find the following: "I would say now 80 percent of the events that happen on campus are hoaxes or pranks." Laird Wilcox, author of the book *Crying Wolf: Hate Crime Hoaxes in America*, told *Fox News*, "It's a place where consciousness of discrimination, sexism, and homophobia is at a peak, and when there's nothing happening, and they need something to happen, they can make it happen."[92] (Does Jussie Smollett come to mind?)

In other words, students attending leftist colleges and universities behave as if they have been programmed to play the role of victim – or proletarian. Moreover, they will fake "hate crimes" against themselves or others in order to fulfill the highly valued and highly rewarded role of victim. To be a victim of one who is perceived to be a narrow-minded, bigoted, middle class (bourgeois), Christian, white male, is viewed as the highest possible achievement on campus – dwarfing the achievement of "high quality scientific research and scholarship."

In his article titled, "Hate Crimes And Hoaxes: 10 Campus Stories Debunked In 2017," Caleb Parke of *FoxNews.com*[93] gave examples of numerous campuses hoaxes. (I counted 10 campuses and 13 hoaxes.) The hoaxes and faked hate crimes included a false claim of rape at the University of Virginia in Charlottesville, a self-made racist message by a black cadet at the U.S. Air force Academy, and a self-scratched female at the University of Michigan.

In addition, a black female student at Michigan State University reported a "noose" on campus that turned out to be a lost shoelace. At St. Olaf College a black female student wrote a note to herself that contained the "N-word." At Bowling Green University in Ohio a student "accused the school of harboring an 'active KKK group,' but it turned out the evidence was a piece of lab equipment covered with a white cloth." At this same Ohio campus students falsely claimed that white Trump supporters threw rocks at them. In Queens College in New York City a Pakistani-American student falsely claimed that "three masked men racially assaulted and robbed him."

False claims of victimhood were not limited to students. At Indiana State University a Muslim Associate Professor named Azhar Hussain was arrested for making anti-Muslim threats – against himself! At San Diego State University a Muslim female student wearing a hijab claimed Trump supporters stole her purse, backpack, and then her car – all of which were lies! At Capital University in Ohio a student filed numerous false claims of victimhood over a period of several years. His false claims included a self-written note with "racist and homophobic language," a self-written note with "racial slurs and swastikas," and an attack by a white male – that never happened!

Welcome to America's leftist "social justice" campuses where students are programmed to eagerly embrace proletariat-style victimhood at the hands of bourgeois villains who exist only in their poisoned imaginations! Sadly, even the U.S. Air Force

Academy is not immune! Yes, today being a victim is a highly valued state among college and university students – and their professors!

Unfortunately, hate crime hoaxes are not limited to older adult and young adult leftists. In Woodbridge, Virginia, a 13-year-old girl "said a man cursed at her, grabbed her arm, and then threatened her with a knife before ripping off her hijab." The young girl also claimed that her attacker called her a "terrorist." Adding more drama to her story, she said she was rescued by a passing motorist who caused her attacker to flee when the vehicle slowed to observe the incident. However, a police investigation revealed the young girl had fabricated the entire "hate crime!"[94]

As pointed out by John Sexton of *HotAir.com*, the above story may sound familiar because a few months earlier an 11-year-old girl in Canada claimed that a man "tried to cut off her hijab" as she walked to Pauline Johnson Junior Public School in Scarborough, Ontario. The young girl said, "I felt really scared and confused." Her hate crime report sparked a press conference and numerous people, including the Mayor of Toronto and Prime Minister Trudeau, rightfully condemned this type of behavior.

"The girl gave an on-camera interview describing the attack in detail. Her mother also made a tearful appearance at the press conference saying, 'I don't know why he did that, but it's just not Canada.' Toronto police announced they were investigating the incident as a hate crime." Unfortunately, a few days later the police reported that the entire ordeal was a hate crime hoax![95, 96]

Today, American and Canadian girls learn to embrace the leftist value of victimhood at an early age! It has such high value among leftists that they are quite willing to lie to achieve that status! Yes, Dr. Thomas Sowell is correct: The brainwashing begins at a very early age in elementary schools across America – and apparently in Canada as well!

While all the above hoaxes were launched against fictitious individuals, the more horrendous hoaxes have been launched by females against real people – with toxic leftist females targeting innocent men and boys!

An Example Of Female Teenage Virtual Manchurian Candidates

This is truly a horrific story!

As reported by Brianna Heldt of *Townhall.com*,[97] a 17-year-old male student (known only as T.F.) at Seneca Valley High School in a northern suburb of Pittsburgh, Pennsylvania, was forced to live a nightmare as a result of numerous false charges of sexual assault launched against him by several female students.

Firstly, a teenage girl (known only as K.S.) falsely claimed that T.F. sexually assaulted her in 2017 while he worked as a life-guard. When later questioned why she filed this false allegation against the young boy, she said, "I just don't like him!" Before she launched this false claim she reportedly said "she would do anything to get [the boy] expelled."

Secondly, another young girl named Megan Villegas, who worked at the pool where T.F. was a lifeguard, falsely claimed that she witnessed the assault by T.F. against K.S. This second girl, Megan Villegas, is a graduate of Seneca Valley High School and a friend of K.S.

Thirdly, in March of 2018 another female student (known only as C.S.) falsely claimed that T.F. came into her home against her will and proceeded to sexually assault her. Fourthly, two other female students (known only as E.S. and H.R.) corroborated the false claim of sexual assault made by C.S.

Following the first false allegation of sexual assault T.F. was charged with indecent assault, two counts of harassment, and placed on six months probation. Following the second false charge against him this innocent young man faced a second charge of indecent assault, criminal trespass, and simple assault. He was subsequently arrested by law enforcement, expelled from school, placed in a juvenile detention center, and eventually placed under house arrest.

In May of 2018 three of the five girls admitted that they fabricated false claims against this male high school student. As Brianna Heldt reported, "And for some reason, Butler County District Attorney Richard Goldinger waited until August 30 to dismiss the second allegation, and September 10 to close the charges of the first."

In addition, this innocent young man was often subjected to bullying by fellow classmates and labeled a "predator" at school. T.F. was subsequently home-schooled for his own protection. T.F.'s parents, Michael J. and Alecia Flood of Zelienople, Butler County, Pennsylvania, hired attorney Craig Fishman and filed a lawsuit against the parents of the five girls, Butler County District Attorney Richard Goldinger's office, and the Seneca Valley School District.

According to *The Associated Press*, "The lawsuit alleges that the boy was further damaged by 'gender bias' by school officials and Goldinger's office, which even after learning the girls' accusations were false 'did not take any action against the females involved,' said attorney Craig Fishman of Pittsburgh, who represents the Floods."[98, 99]

"(T.F.) was basically being tortured in school by the other students and investigators, but the administration was only focused on protecting the girls who were lying," Fishman said. "Once the allegations were proven false, they really didn't care one bit about T.F. and there has [sic] been absolutely no repercussions against the girls."[100]

As a consequence of this horrendous ordeal, young T.F. has been in psychological counseling to help him deal with the physical and emotional impact of being falsely accused of sexual assault on two occasions by five teenage girls who, according to attorney Craig Fishman, conspired to launch false allegations of sexual misconduct against him!

Welcome to leftist America, complete with well-programmed and well-protected female teenage character assassins. It is a world where young people are taught the well-honored leftist Commandment that is routinely obeyed by leftist politicians, lawyers, judges, journalists, reporters, educators, and even religious leaders: "Thou shalt bear false witness against thy neighbor!" If these five young girls attend leftist "social justice" colleges and universities after they graduate from high school, they will certainly be groomed and programmed to excel as Virtual Manchurian Candidates!

Then someday they, too, may join Christine Fair, a professor at Georgetown University, who stated the following regarding the Republican men at the Dr. Ford/Judge Kavanaugh hearing: "Look at thus chorus of entitled white men justifying a serial rapist's arrogated entitlement. All of them deserve miserable deaths while feminists laugh as they take their last gasps. Bonus: we castrate their corpses and feed them to swine? Yes."[101]

How does the moral maturity of this leftist professor stack up against Judge Kavanaugh's young daughter who said they should pray for her father's accuser?

We may also ask, how many students, past and present, have been groomed to follow in the footsteps of the special education teacher in Rosemount, Minnesota who was caught threatening the life of Judge Brett Kavanaugh shortly after he was sworn in as Justice Brett Kavanaugh? The name of the special education teacher at the Intermediate School District 917's Alliance Education Center who made the threat has not been revealed. The teacher was initially placed on paid leave pending an investigation by school district officials, and she resigned shortly thereafter. The threat was made in the form of a tweet wherein she wrote, "So whose [sic] gonna take one for the team and kill Kavanaugh?" Concerned citizens notified the FBI of her threat.[102]

Democrats Repeatedly Introduced Anti-White Racism Into The Nonracial Ford/Kavanagh Controversy

As alluded to on pages 91 and 92, leftists inject race into a discussion when race is not relevant to the topic at hand. For example, although Dr. Ford and Judge Kavanaugh are both white, leftists still injected race into that controversy. Why? Because under classical Marxism we find the proletariat versus the bourgeoisie, and under Cultural Marxism in America, leftist feminists represent one proletariat group while conservative white males represent the bourgeoisie – especially if they are Bible-based, Christian white males – such as Judge Kavanaugh.

Thus, defending Judge Kavanaugh against a leftist lynch mob can be portrayed as an example of defending "white privilege." White male senators would thus be defending a "white privilege" judge – and both represent "bourgeoisie privilege."

As reported in the headline of the *Washington Examiner*, "Media convict Brett Kavanaugh and GOP on grounds of being white males." In this article Eddie Scarry wrote, "To the media, that Kavanaugh is a white man and that the Republicans in control of the Judiciary Committee are all also white men is a problem to correct, thus it's repeated over and over again on its own, without context as to why anyone should care."[103]

Welcome to the racist, misandrist world of the toxic leftist feminist proletariat founded by Betty Friedan and now inhabited by Dr. Christine Blasey Ford, Christine Fair, and countless other "social justice warriors."

Recall the following facts presented earlier in this book: The Women's March chastised Republican white women for not voting in greater numbers for corrupt Democrat politicians. Ana Cabrera of CNN falsely claimed that "President Trump and his son Don Jr. said this week white men have a lot to fear right now." But neither President Trump nor his son mentioned race when discussing the issue of false allegations of sexual mis-conduct against men. At Bowling Green University in Ohio campus students falsely claimed that white Trump supporters threw rocks at them. At Capital University in Ohio a student filed numerous false claims of victimhood over a period of several years. His false claims included a self-written note with "racist and homophobic language," a self-written note with "racial slurs and swastikas," and an attack by a white male – that never happened!

And as just noted, Christine Fair, a professor at Georgetown University, stated the following regarding the Republican men at the Dr. Ford/Judge Kavanaugh hearing: "Look at thus chorus of entitled white men justifying a serial rapist's arrogated entitle-ment. All of them deserve miserable deaths while feminists laugh as they take their last gasps. Bonus: we castrate their corpses and feed them to swine? Yes."

We may also ask, why did a black female motorist file a vicious, false allegation of racism against a polite and innocent white male police officer? Why did a black female exotic dancer file false allegations of rape against white male Duke Lacrosse players? Why did Tawana Brawley, a black female, file false charges of rape against white males in New York? (Visit *HotAir.com*[104] and review the list of fake anti-black and fake anti-gay hate crimes lodged primarily against imaginary "Trump supporters." Similar lists have been complied by others.)

This book is not about race, but in examining the topic of Dr. Christine Blasey Ford's allegation against Judge Brett Kavanaugh – again, both of whom are white – we find that the supporters of Dr. Ford kept injecting anti-white racist remarks into the discussion. And black females falsely accuse white males of racism or sexual assault and white females falsely accuse white men of sexual misconduct. While this author explains leftist anti-white racism and anti-male sexism from the classical Marxist perspective, Ann Coulter wrote, "Today, 'white supremacy' is nothing but a comfortable fantasy the Left developed to explain its sick preoccupation with white people." And, "When will we get around to talking about the media's actual hatred of whites?"[105]

Would A Woman Lie To The Senate Judiciary Committee About Rape – While Under Oath?

Answer: Yes!

If you, the reader, have concluded that no woman would be so bold as to profusely lie under oath to a Senate Judiciary

Committee regarding an alleged sexual assault, think again! All or nearly all of the information Dr. Ford provided regarding the alleged attack by Judge Brett Kavanaugh has proven to be contradictory, unverifiable, uncorroborated, or flat out refuted. When seeking to determine if she is often confused or often deceitful, keep in mind that if she lied, she would not have been the first woman to have lied to the Senate Judiciary Committee regarding an alleged sexual assault.

The reader is encouraged to examine an article at *Townhall.com* by Phelim McAleer, titled, "Flashback: Woman Lies About Being Raped to the Senate Judiciary Committee."[106] I got a chill up my spine when I saw the uncanny similarities between the behavior of Jamie Leigh Jones and that of Dr. Christine Blasey Ford. Both women appeared before the Senate Judiciary committee; both women claimed to be victims of sexual assault; both gave conflicting information and provided information that was later refuted by others; both women failed to provide evidence or corroborating witnesses, and both women appeared before a committee that was inhabited by Senators Feinstein, Klobuchar, Durbin, Leahy, and Whitehouse – all of whom sympathized with both women.

Briefly, "In 2009, Jamie Leigh Jones told the Committee that four years earlier, on her second night working in Iraq for Halliburton subsidiary KBR (Kellogg, Brown & Root), her drink was spiked at a party and she was gang-raped by a group of Halliburton-employed American firefighters."

While the fate of Dr. Ford remains to be seen, a jury found the allegations of Jamie Leigh Jones to be not credible. As Phelim MaAleer noted, "Jones asked the jury for $145 million in the Halliburton trial. Instead, in a virtually unprecedented decision, the jury found against her and made her pay $145,000 in legal costs to KBR."

So, although Jamie Leigh Jones was apparently believed by sympathetic Democrat senators, she was not believed by a jury that looked objectively at the evidence – and the lack of it! Unlike leftist politicians, journalists, and other leftist political activists, jury members were not motivated by ulterior political motives to believe her, to present her as a credible victim, or to smear the characters of those who were falsely accused.

One Kavanaugh Accuser
Admitted That She Lied

While Judge Brett Kavanaugh's character was under assault from numerous leftist women, a left-wing political activist, who is decades older than Judge Brett Kavanaugh, falsely claimed that he had sexually assaulted her. The accuser, named Judy Munro-Leighton, initially said that she was the author of the "Jane Doe" letter wherein the claim was made. However, "Jane Doe" lived in Oceanside, California, but accuser Judy Munro-Leighton lived in Kentucky. She admitted that she "just wanted to get attention," and further admitted that she had never met Judge Kavanaugh.

Katie Pavlich of *Townhall.com* wrote, "According to a letter sent to Attorney General Jeff Sessions late Friday afternoon, Senate Judiciary Committee Chairman Chuck Grassley referred Judy Munro-Leighton for criminal prosecution and revealed her actions were part of a ploy to take down Kavanaugh's nomination."[107]

Another Example Demonstrating
The Leftist Lynch Mob Mentality Against
Men & Boys Has Infected Canada As Well

There is a *Youtube.com* video titled, *Boys are guilty even when innocent*. In the video we learn that in Ottawa, Canada, two young adult women met two men in a bar back in the year 2003. The two women left the bar with the two men, and later had sex with the men that night. The next day the women charged the men with rape. Following an investigation, the police could find no evidence of rape, and there were no witnesses. The men admitted having sex with the two women, but claimed it was consensual. The women, the leftist media, and various activists criticized the police for not charging the men with rape.

Just like their American counterparts, men are guilty of a crime simply because some women say they are guilty. No evidence is necessary! No witnesses are necessary! The presumption of innocence until proven guilty no longer applies to men when the accuser is a woman! The men may be guilty or they may be innocent. There is no way to know in the absence of evidence and witnesses! But in this case, like other cases, the two women who claimed to be victims, the reporters, and various activists, all wanted the two men arrested, tried, convicted, and imprisoned when there was no evidence that a crime had been committed. They falsely believe that being guilty under public opinion is the same as being guilty under the law. How sad! How frightening![108]

While there was no evidence of a crime in this particular case, there is, however, abundance evidence to support Christina Hoff Sommers' contention that we are witnessing *The War Against Boys!* Her book was published back in 2001, and becomes more relevant as each year passes.

The number of examples of false allegations of abuse lodged by leftists against innocent people or fictitious people seems endless. However, if you wish to explore a few more interesting examples, consider the following:

Sophie Skinner, a 25-year-old female from Woodland Crescent, Llanfoist, Wales, falsely accused an 18-year old man of rape. The young man, Damon Osborne, admitted having sex with Skinner, but said it was consensual. The young man spent 17 hours in police custody and was subjected to "embarrassing" medical examinations. He was given a curfew when on bail, which impacted his work and social life. He lost one job because the curfew forbade him from working the hours required by the employer.

Unfortunately for accuser Sophie Skinner, closed circuit television revealed that she had initiated the sexual activity. Damon Osborne stated that, "I knew I was innocent but it didn't stop me thinking about the worst case scenario and being sent to prison for something I didn't do." He added, "If there was no CCTV in this case she may have been believed and I would be spending years in prison. It would have ruined my life."[109]

On the tenth anniversary of the March, 2006, Duke Lacrosse gang rape hoax, Mary Katharine Ham wrote an eye-opening article. In this case three white male lacrosse players at Duke University were falsely accused of gang rape by a black female exotic dancer. As we saw with the allegations against Judge Brett Kavanaugh, in the Duke Lacrosse case leftist journalists, politicians, professors, and other activists all found it impossible to think logically and unemotionally. Why? Because the accused students were white and male while the hoaxer was black and female. In Marxist terms, the accused belonged to two bourgeois groups and the fake victim belonged to two proletariat groups!

As we saw with the Judge Kavanaugh leftist lynch mob, the leftist media found the young men guilty with no evidence, a coach was fired for supporting his innocent players, and due process was abandoned by the politicians and Duke University professors. Mary Katharine Ham concluded that "...the falsely accused players showed more maturity than their professors and the media."

She added, "To this day [March 16, 2016], most of the Duke faculty and leadership who prejudged the lacrosse players remain in their positions and have never apologized. Media figures who apologized or retracted are few and far between. Instead, most coverage offered grudging reporting on the dismissal of charges."[110]

Nikki Yovino, a student at Sacred Heart University in Connecticut, told police that two football players from the same university had trapped her in a bathroom at a party and raped her. The two young men admitted having sex with the young woman, but stated that it was consensual. She stuck to her story – until others came forward to support the story of the two young men.

Unlike most female false accusers, Nikki Yovino was charged with falsely reporting a rape and "tampering or fabricated physical evidence." Prosecutors were seeking a six year prison term, but before the case went to trial, she made a plea deal that resulted in a one year sentence. As a student at a Catholic university, one would expect Nikki Yovino to be familiar with the Ten Commandments – and not flagrantly violate the ninth!

According to Jazz Shaw of *HotAir.com*, "This is, quite frankly, shocking, to say the least. We're so conditioned to never do anything to upset a sexual assault victim that even when one is proven to be completely false, nothing ever seems to happen to them. (Has anyone noticed 'Jackie' from the Rolling Stone story being marched off in handcuffs yet?)" [111, 112]

An unnamed woman claimed that four California dentists repeatedly raped her at Wynn Las Vegas. The four men were charged with sexual assault, conspiracy to commit sexual assault, and kidnapping. However, prosecutors dropped all charges, according to attorney Robert Draskovich, "After a review of the facts of the case, it was clear that the allegations were completely fabricated." He further stated that, "The (video) evidence confirmed the men's innocence, and the state has cleared them of all charges."[113]

In a really bizarre case, a white adult female falsely claimed that a nine-year-old black boy groped her in a Brooklyn, New York deli. She dialed 911 and the police responded. But the video footage showed that the boy's backpack "grazed her backside," according to Matt Vespa of *Townhall.com*. Initially, Teresa Klein, the 53-year-old accuser, said "I was sexually assaulted by a child." She also stated that "The son grabbed my ass and she (the mother of the child) decided to yell at me." When Teresa Klein returned to the store later and reviewed the video footage, she apologized to the young boy.[114]

40 Percent Of Sexual Assault Charges May Be False!

While Dr. Christine Blasey Ford and other women were accusing Judge Brett Kavanaugh of sexual misconduct, the Democrat Media Smear Machine repeatedly gave a fake statistic to make the accusers appear legitimate and the accused appear guilty. As reported by Rowan Scarborough at *WashingtonTimes.com*, during the confirmation process media leftists repeatedly reported that only two percent of allegations of sexual misconduct turn out to be false. But this is a fake statistic. One study placed the figure at 40 percent. Scarborough noted that, "Conservative commentator Michelle Malkin says the two percent number was one of the most frequent weapons unleashed against Justice Kavanaugh, who was confirmed and sworn in on Saturday."[115]

Scarborough based his article on a 2017 book co-authored by a criminologist named Brent E. Turvey. The book is titled *False Allegations: Investigative and Forensic Issues in Fraudulent Reports of Crime*. In his book Mr. Turvey provides 10 studies that debunked the two percent statistic. While the National Sexual Violence Resource Center reports that two to 10 percent of allegations of sexual assault are false, other studies range from 18 to 40 percent. So why did the Democrat Media Smear Machine hide this information from the public and continue to chant the two percent mantra? I believe Michelle Malkin was correct: Leftists used the fake figure of two percent as a weapon against Judge Brett Kavanaugh!

It's 'A Very Frightening Time' For Men

Attorney Andrew Miltenberg reported that he has defended "hundreds" of young men who were charged with sexual abuse. Most of the cases he handled occurred within university set-tings. According to Miltenberg, "In most cases – not all – women are seeking revenge on ex-boyfriends or young men they found have played around too much." He added, "It's very difficult for young men to get a fair opportunity to be heard."[116]

As noted earlier, following the unsubstantiated charges of sexual misconduct against Judge Brett Kavanaugh, President Trump said, "It's a very scary time for young men in America, where you can be guilty of something that you may not be guilty of." President Trump was also speaking from personal experience, given that several women have made allegations of sexual mis-conduct against him – all of which he has denied.

Miltenberg agreed with President Trump and said, "It's a very frightening time" for men. He added, "I don't really believe you can be alone in a room with a young woman now in this climate" given that a man can have his life and career destroyed by false

134

allegations of sexual misconduct. Thus, Miltenberg not only agrees with President Trump on this topic, he also agrees with Vice President Mike Pence who wisely will not allow himself to be with another woman unless his wife is present. Both Vice President Pence and his wife understand the threat posed by the toxic leftist feminist proletariat and their pathological bigotry against bourgeois males! If up to 40 percent of sexual assault charges may be false, how many innocent males are now sitting in prison for sex crimes they did not commit?

Should All Men And Boys Wear Body Cameras?

Body cameras have become commonplace among law enforce officers, and sometimes those cameras expose false allegations of abuse by dishonest motorists. For example, as reported by Michael Barnes of *LibertyHeadlines.com* (and alluded to earlier), in Brunswick County, Virginia, a black female motorist was pulled over and ticketed by a white male police officer.

She later posted a Facebook video that contained the following: "I was just bullied by a racist cop, who threatened to pull me out of the car. This is where we got lynched. This is where we got lynched, even in today's day." The Facebook video went viral and caught the attention of the Brunswick County Sheriff's Department, which released the body camera footage of the entire incident. Unfortunately for this false accuser, the footage showed the police officer handling the situation in a polite and professional manner.[117]

Why did this black woman file a vicious, false allegation of racism against a polite and innocent white male police officer? Where did she learn this despicable behavior? Perhaps now we may ask, should all men and boys wear body cameras? What would have happened to the career of this police officer if he had not been wearing a body camera? Clearly, his reputation and perhaps his career could have been ruined – based on a vicious lie!

Remember Damon Osborne of Wales who was falsely accused of rape? He was found innocent because of closed circuit television and he stated the following: "I knew I was innocent but it didn't stop me thinking about the worst case scenario and being sent to prison for something I didn't do. If there was no CCTV in this case she may have been believed and I would be spending years in prison. It would have ruined my life."

What about the 53-year-old white woman who falsely accused a nine-year-old black boy of grouping her behind. The boy was saved by the deli security video which showed the boy's back-pack accidentally rubbed up against the woman's backside. What would have happened to the four California dentists who were falsely accused of gang rape if a security video had not clearly shown that the accuser was lying?

In the age of toxic leftist feminism, perhaps all men and boys should wear body cameras. Then men like Vice President Mike Pence could safely eat lunch with women other than his wife without his wife or some other reliable witness being present. (And leftists who promote toxic leftist feminism criticize or mock VP Pence for his justifiably cautious behavior – justified by the epidemic of false victimhood created by leftists!)[118, 119, 120]

Which Side Do Witches Support?

You may recall that after Donald Trump defeated Hillary Clinton in the 2016 presidential election, leftists across the nation were in a state of shock. Leftist feminists were seen sobbing on our TV screens. Joining in their grief were countless witches from far and wide. In early February it was reported that witches planned to cast a spell on the newly elected president. Beginning on February 24, 2017, a "mass spell to bind Donald Trump" was performed at midnight and will be performed during every waning crescent moon, "until Donald Trump is removed from office."

The spell performed by the witches consisted of a lengthy incantation wherein they called upon spirits and "demons of the infernal realms" to bind President Trump so that "he may fail utterly, that he may do no harm." The witches' spell also invoked evil upon "those who abet" President Trump. This, of course, would include his family, White House staff, cabinet members, politicians, and the tens of millions of voters who supported Donald Trump for the presidency. To counter the work of the witches, Bible-based Christian groups and individuals made a commitment to pray for President Trump and the nation.[121, 122, 123]

A few days after Judge Kavanaugh became Justice Kavanaugh, witches and warlocks in New York City organized a huge rally that was held on October 20, 2018. What was the purpose of the rally? The purpose was to place a "hex" on the newest member of the U.S. Supreme Court! Members of the public were invited to attend while the witches and warlocks placed a "hex on Brett Kavanaugh, upon all rapists and the patriarchy at large which emboldens, rewards and protects them."

In the 1990s Juanita Broaddrick claimed that Bill Clinton raped her – twice – in 1978! I wonder if New York City witches and warlocks held a similar ritual after he was elected president? Or did they follow the example set by Senator Diane Feinstein and ignore her allegation of rape against Bill Clinton?[124, 125]

As reported by Timothy Meads of *Townhall.com*,[126] "The event costs $10 per person. 50% of profits will go towards two organizations; The Ali Forney Center and Planned Parenthood.

The Ali Ford Center is a nonprofit assisting homeless LGBT youths. Planned Parenthood is an organization that kills more than 320,000 babies each year." While the witches who condemned Justice Brett Kavanaugh donated to abortion provider Planned Parenthood, *National Right To Life News Today* wrote, "National Right to Life Commends President Trump For His Selection of Judge Brett Kavanaugh as Successor to Justice Kennedy."[127]

After learning that witches were planning to place a hex on Justice Brett Kavanaugh, who is a practicing Roman Catholic, Father Gary Thomas, a California priest, announced that he would hold a mass for the new U.S. Supreme Court Justice. Father Gary Thomas is no ordinary priest, he is an exorcist for the Diocese of San Jose, California. Aris Folley of *TheHill.com* also noted that, "A wider group of Catholics and exorcists also plan to pray and fast for 'the protection' of Kavanaugh..."[128]

So, in Hillary Rodham Clinton versus Donald J. Trump in the 2016 presidential election, witches supported Hillary Clinton – and convened to "bind" Donald Trump after his victory over Hillary – their political leader. In Dr. Ford versus Justice Kavanaugh witches supported Dr. Ford in the 2018 hearings – and convened to put a "hex" on Justice Kavanaugh after his victory over Dr. Ford – their political ally. Do you see a trend developing here? Why are witches consistently supporting Democrats and casting spells on Republicans? Why do Bible-based Christians support President Donald Trump and Justice Brett Kavanaugh while witches support Hillary Clinton and Dr. Ford?

Which side do you support?

Democrats Are Fake Defenders
Of Women And Children!

"I just can't grasp having the kind of mindset it takes to completely ignore such violent and heinous acts, especially against children." – James Johnson, President, North Carolinians for Immigration Reform and Enforcement[129]

Democrats portray themselves as the protectors of women and children, but hard evidence exposes that falsehood. During his January 8, 2019 address to the nation regarding the need for a southern border security wall, President Trump[130] stated the following: "In the last two years, ICE officers made 266,000 arrests of aliens with criminal records, including those charged or convicted of 100,000 assaults, **30,000 sex crimes**, and 4,000 violent killings. Over the years, thousands of Americans have been brutally killed by those who illegally entered our country, and thousands more lives will be lost if we don't act right now."

Keep in mind that most sex crimes are not reported by victims. According to *Rainn.org*,[131] roughly three out of every four sexual assaults are not reported to law enforcement. The National Research Council[132] estimates that only 20 percent, or one in five sexual assaults, are reported to law enforcement. So the actual number of **sex crimes committed by illegal aliens** in America in the last two years may be as high as **120,000** or even **150,000**. Why do Democrats turn their backs on these victims?

Where are the Soros-financed protesters? Where is the leftist Women's March? Where is NOW? Where are the ABC, CBS, NBC, MSNBC, and CNN investigative reporters? Where are the witches and warlocks? Where are the supporters of Dr. Christine Blasey Ford? Where are the 1,600 leftist signatories in *The New York Times*? Where is Diane Feinstein? Where is Nancy Pelosi? Where is Chuck Schumer? Where are the defenders of the thousands of sex crime victims that are created each year in America by illegal aliens?

You won't find any defenders among the above leftist individuals or groups! However, you will find the defenders of these countless, nameless, sex crime victims in the political party of Abraham Lincoln, Ronald Reagan, Donald Trump, Clarence Thomas, and Brett Kavanaugh!

Where are Democrats on this issue?

Firstly, the Democrat media and Democrat politicians and activists hide this vital life-and-death information from the American people. For example, Joshua Paladino of *Liberty-Headlines.com*[133] reported that, "In 2018, more than 200 illegal aliens committed nearly 750 acts of child rape or child sexual assault in North Carolina." James Johnson, President of North Carolinians for Immigration Reform and Enforcement stated that more than 315 media outlets as well as numerous elected public officials in North Carolina receive "monthly child rape reports."

What is their response? "Crickets," says Johnson. He further stated that, "I just can't grasp having the kind of mindset it takes to completely ignore such violent and heinous acts, especially against children." Unfortunately, far too many Americans seem unwilling or unable to acknowledge that we are witnessing the mindset of people in the media and in public office who are truly evil – but portray themselves as morally superior to the people who sincerely want to protect women and children from illegal alien predators!

This "See no evil, hear no evil, say no evil" attitude of truly evil people has infected leftist media outlets and leftist politicians nationwide! Michael Barnes of *LibertyHeadlines.com* reported on a press conference held by Republican politicians who were flanked by "Angel Moms," – women who have lost children at the hands of illegal aliens. Congressman Mo Brooks, an Alabama Republican, noted that the media gave weeklong coverage to the deaths of two children of illegal alien parents who died at the U.S-Mexican border. However, this same media completely ignore the thousands of American children who are sexually assaulted or killed at the hands of illegal aliens each year.

Congressman Brooks said, "Wouldn't it be nice if CNN, MSNBC, ABC, CBS, NBC, the *Washington Post* and the *New York Times* to tell their stories [of Angel Moms] the way they told the stories of the two illegal alien children who died?" Brooks added, "What you're seeing today is just a microcosm of what is happening across America."[134]

Secondly, Democrats are actually leading the fight **against** border security – and some even advocate abolishing ICE and maintaining open borders – which would drive the number of violent crimes committed by illegal aliens to a level that only a psychopath could love! So, why do Democrat women vote "against the best interest" of these sex crime victims? Clearly, the leftist Women's March is shamefully wrong: It's the Democrat women who have "a lot of learning" and "a lot of growing" to do – not Republican white women!

Thirdly, Democrats smear anyone who wants to prevent violent foreign criminals from illegally entering the U.S. Often they are falsely labeled as "racists." The supporters of border security clearly fall into Hillary Clinton's "Basket of Deplorables" which, as noted earlier, she described as "racist, sexist, homophobic, xenophobic, Islamophobic, you name it."

Democrats will also cite numerous flawed studies that indicate illegal aliens commit fewer crimes than natural-born American citizens. According to the Pew Research Center,[135] there were about 10.7 million illegal aliens in America in 2016, and they represent about 3.3 percent of the U.S. population. However, according to the U.S. Department of Homeland Security,[136] 23 percent of the federal prison inmates were illegal aliens in 2017. If illegal aliens commit fewer crimes than natural-born American citizens, they would make up less than 3.3 percent of the federal prison population – not the current 23 percent! If you double the number of illegal aliens to 21.4 million, that still represents only 6.6 percent of the U.S. population.

Many leftists falsely claim that security walls don't work. However, as Wayne Allyn Root[137] has noted, "Facts prove the Israeli wall works. The number of terror attacks has been reduced by 99 percent." And, "As a bonus, Israel says illegal immigration has been completely halted. According to *The Jerusalem Post*, illegal immigration dropped from 9,500 in the six months before the wall was completed to 36 – and eventually to zero. And drug smuggling has been dramatically reduced, too."

Clearly, Democrats don't care about women – they only care about the female vote! They don't care about children – unless they can abort them! They don't care about sex crime victims – unless they can exploit them for political purposes! They don't care about national security and they certainly don't care about truth. They only care about power – financial and political power – regardless of the cost to others!

Democrats Say "Security For Me, But Not For Thee!"

"Every crime committed by an illegal alien is one that would not have occurred if that alien wasn't in the United States in the first place." – Hans A. von Spakovsky and Grant Strobl, *Heritage-.org*.[138]

Wayne Allyn Root noted that former Democrat Senator Harry Reid lives in Anthem Country Club in Nevada. It is an exclusive area for very wealthy people. The entire community of 1,500 expensive homes is surrounded by a high security wall, has armed security guards at the front gate, and requires a government-issued photo ID card for entrance.[139]

So, while this elitist Democrat opposes a public security wall to protect poor and middle class Americans, he protects himself and his family behind a private security wall. Like nearly all elitist Democrats, he believes that wealthy people should be protected by armed private security guards, but poor and middle class Americans should not be protected by armed family members who cannot afford armed private security guards! Like nearly all elitist Democrats, he believes that wealthy people should be protected against fraud by requiring government-issued photo ID cards for poor and middle class workers who enter their property, but American voters should not be protected against voter fraud by requiring government-issued photo ID cards for poor and middle class people who enter the voting booth.

In his article Wayne Allyn Root listed the names of many leftist elitists who share Harry Reid's "Security for me, but not for thee" attitude. Why does anyone vote for these two-faced hypocrites who protect themselves and the women and children in their families – but deny you your natural right to protect yourself and the women and children in your family? Perhaps Dr. Sebastian Gorka was correct when he stated on his *America First* radio program (January 24, 2019) that, "If the Left didn't have double standards, they would have no standards at all."

∞ ∞ ∞

"Things my Democrat women colleagues wouldn't clap for at #StateOfTheUnion2019 tonight: America, freedom, free enterprise, law enforcement heroes, record low unemployment for women & minorities, the right of babies to live. Things they did clap for: themselves." – Liz Cheney, February 6, 2019, Tweet[140]

143

Chapter One References

1. Caroline Hallemann, "Read the Full Transcript of Christine Blasey Ford's Opening Statement at Brett Kavanaugh's Hearing," *TownAndCountryMag.com*, September 27, 2018.

2. Ibid.

3. John Haltiwanger, "Kavanaugh delivers fiery, emotional opening remarks in Senate hearing, claims his life has been 'totally and permanently destroyed,'" *BusinessInsider.com*, September 27, 2018.

4. Emma Brown, "California professor, writer of confidential Brett Kavanaugh letter, speaks out about her allegation of sexual assault," *WashingtonPost.com*, September 16, 2018.

5. Daniel Chaitin, "Read the summer 1982 calendar Brett Kavanaugh gave to the Senate Judiciary Committee," *Washing-tonExaminer.com*, September 26, 2018.

6. Kylie Handler, "Top Kavanaugh accuser's testimony derailed Tuesday?" *TheHornNews.com*, October 3, 2018.

7. Transcript courtesy of Bloomberg Government, "Kavanaugh hearing: Transcript," *WashingtonPost.com*, September 27, 2018.

8. Mollie Hemmingway, "Analyzing the media coverage of Judge Brett Kavanaugh," *Life, Liberty & Levin, YouTube.com, Fox News* Channel, October 7, 2018.

9. Kylie Handler, "Top Kavanaugh accuser's testimony derailed Tuesday?" *TheHornNews.com*, October 3, 2018.

10. Ibid.

11. Christal Hayes, "Here's the polygraph test Christine Blasey Ford took on her allegations against Kavanaugh," *USAtoday.com*, September 26, 2018.

12. Guy Benson, "Discrepancy: Kavanaugh Accuser Has Said She Was Attacked in the 'Mid-1980's' and in Her 'Late Teens,' Differing From Her Account," *Townhall.com*, October 1, 2018.

13. Christal Hayes, "Here's the polygraph test Christine Blasey Ford took on her allegations against Kavanaugh," *USAtoday.com*, September 26, 2018.

14. Steve Straub, "Margot Cleveland Eviscerates Blasey-Ford's Testimony; Lays Out The Case," *TheFederalistPapers.org*, October 1, 2018.

15. Transcript courtesy of Bloomberg Government, "Kavanaugh hearing: Transcript," *WashingtonPost.com*, September 27, 2018.

16. John Nolte, "Prosecutor's senate report outlines 9 reasons why Christine Blasey Ford not credible," *Breitbart.com*, October 1, 2018.

17. Bart Marcois, "Just How Good Was That Ford Polygraph?" *Opslens.com*, September 27, 2018.

18. "New Details Raise Serious Doubts Over the Credibility Of The Ford Polygraph," *JonathanTurley.org*, September 27, 2018.

19. Matt Naham, "This is the Most Meaningless Proof of Christine Ford's Truthfulness Out There Right Now," *LawAndCrime.com*, September 19, 2018.

20. Ibid.

21. Dick Morris, "How I Helped to Save Judge Kavanaugh," (Video), *DickMorris.com*, January 14, 2018.

22. Terresa Monroe-Hamilton, "Breaking: Dr. Ford's Polygraph Scam Exposed – She Should Be Arrested," *RWNofficial.com*, October 3, 2018.

23. Erin Kelly, "Brett Kavanaugh's friend Mark Judge declines to testify about alleged sexual assault," *USAtoday.com*, September 18, 2018.

24. Daniel Payne, "3 big questions hanging after Christine Blasey Ford's testimony on Brett Kavanaugh," *USAtoday.com*, October 1, 2018.

25. Naomi Lim, "Former Kavanaugh Classmate "PJ" Smyth has 'truthfully answered' all FBI questions, lawyer says," *WashingtonExaminer.com*, October 1, 2018.

26. John Nolte, "Prosecutor's senate report outlines 9 reasons why Christine Blasey Ford not credible," *Breitbart.com*, October 1, 2018.

27. Guy Benson, "Kavanaugh's Accuser Named Four Other Attendees at the Alleged Party. All Four Have Now Contradicted Her Story," *Townhall.com*, September 9, 2018.

28. Gabriella Munoz, "Leland Keyser felt pressured by friends to make clear she believed Ford's allegation: Report," *WashingtonTimes.com*, October 5, 2018.

29. Guy Benson, "Kavanaugh's Accuser Named Four Other Attendees at the Alleged Party. All Four Have Now Contradicted Her Story," *Townhall.com*, September 24, 2018.

30. Guy Benson, "Unraveled: How a Democratic Senator's Theory About Kavanaugh's 1982 Calendar Totally Fell Apart," *Townhall.com*, October 1, 2018.

31. Guy Benson, "Kavanaugh's Accuser Named Four Other Attendees at the Alleged Party. All Four Have Now Contradicted Her Story," *Townhall.com*, September 24, 2018.

32. Paul Sperry, "Eight big problems for Christine Blasey Ford's story," *NYpost.com*, September 25, 2018.

33. Ibid.

34. Phillip Klein, "Rachel Mitchell's memo is damaging to Christine Blasey Ford's case against Brett Kavanaugh," *WashingtonExaminer.com*, October 1, 2018.

35. Gregg Re, John Roberts, "Christine Blasey Ford ex-boyfriend says she helped friend prep for potential polygraph; Grassley sounds alarm," *FoxNews.com*, October 3, 2018.

36. John Nolte, "Nolte: New Evidence Eliminates Christine Blasey Ford's Residual Credibility," *Breitbart.com*, October 3, 2018.

37. Gregg Re, John Roberts, "Christine Blasey Ford ex-boyfriend says she helped friend prep for potential polygraph; Grassley sounds alarm," *FoxNews.com*, October 3, 2018.

38. Ashley (Kimber), "EVERYONE Should Read This FASCINATING Breakdown Of Blasey Ford's Testimony," *ChicksOnRight.com*, October 1, 2018.

39. John Nolte, "Prosecutor's senate report outlines 9 reasons why Christine Blasey Ford not credible," *Breitbart.com*, October 1, 2018.

40. Margot Cleveland, "Christine Blasey Ford's changing Kavanaugh assault story leaves her short on credibility," *USAtoday.com*, October 3, 2018.

41. Ibid.

42. Ashley (Kimber), "EVERYONE Should Read This FASCINATING Breakdown Of Blasey Ford's Testimony," *ChicksOnRight.com*, October 1, 2018.

43. Ibid.

44. John Nolte, "Prosecutor's senate report outlines 9 reasons why Christine Blasey Ford not credible," *Breitbart.com*, October 1, 2018.

45. Margot Cleveland, "Christine Blasey Ford's changing Kavanaugh assault story leaves her short on credibility," *USAtoday.com*, October 3, 2018.

46. Matt Walsh, "Walsh: How We Know That Christine Ford Is A Liar," *DailyWire.com*, October 3, 2018.

47. Paul Sperry, "Eight big problems for Christine Blasey Ford's story," *NYpost.com*, September 25, 2018.

48. Ibid.

49. John Nolte, "Prosecutor's senate report outlines 9 reasons why Christine Blasey Ford not credible," *Breitbart.com*, October 1, 2018.

50. Emma Brown, "California professor, writer of confidential Brett Kavanaugh letter, speaks out about her allegation of sexual assault," *WashingtonPost.com*, September 16, 2018.

51. Janice Fiamengo, "To Understand Christine Blasey Ford, Take a look at Palo Alto University," The Fiamengo File, Episode 89, StudioBrule, *YouTube.com*, October 6, 2018.

52. Paul Sperry, "Eight big problems for Christine Blasey Ford's story," *NYpost.com*, September 25, 2018.

53. John Nolte, "Prosecutor's senate report outlines 9 reasons why Christine Blasey Ford not credible," *Breitbart.com*, October 1, 2018.

54. Ibid.

55. Brad Slager, "How The Christine Ford Testimony Exposed The Democrat Smear Machine," *RedState.com*, September 28, 2018.

56. Lorie Byrd, "An Important Revelation from Dr. Ford's Testimony," *Townhall.com*, September 30, 2018.

57. Joshua Paladino, "Bar Complaint Filed Against Blasey Ford's Lawyers for Misconduct," *LibertyHeadlines.com*, October 19, 2018.

58. Ben Sellers, "Mitchell Report Reveals Many Holes in Ford's So-Called Credible Testimony," *LibertyHeadlines.com*, October 1, 2018.

59. Nicholas Fandos, "Dianne Feinstein Rode One Court Fight to the Senate. Another Has Left Her Under Siege," *NYtimes.com*, September 21, 2018.

60. The Ingraham Angle, "Gingrich: Dems Displayed 'Most Despicable Behavior By a Major Party in Modern History,'" *Insider.FoxNews.com*, September 27, 2018.

61. Cortney O'Brein, "The latest Demands From Ford," *Town-Hall.com*, September 20, 2018.

62. Miranda Morales, "NEW: Dr. Ford's Attorneys Make More Demands Of Grassley In Letter," *RedState.com*, September 24, 2018.

63. Kerry Picket, 65 Women From Kavanaugh's High School Years Defend Judge In Letter To Senate," *DailyCaller.com*, September 14, 2018.

64. Erin Kelly, "GOP releases summary of FBI report on Kavanaugh: 'No corroboration of the allegations,'" *USA-today.com*, October 5, 2018.

65. Timothy Meads, "American Bar Association Gives Brett Kavanaugh a Unanimous Well-Qualified Rating," *Townhall.com*, August 31, 2018.

66. Joel B. Pollak, "Senate Judiciary Committee Releases Full Brett Kavanaugh Report: 'No Evidence' of Sexual Misconduct," *Breitbart.com*, November 3, 2018.

67. Byron York, "As The World Moves On, The Brett Kavanaugh Fight Continues," *Townhall.com*, November 7, 2018.

68. Caroline Hallemann, "Read the Full Transcript of Brett Kavanaugh's Opening Statement at Today's Hearing," *TownAnd-CountryMag.com*, September 27, 2018.

69. Richard Pollock, "FLASHBACK: Clinton White House Declared War On The Independent Counsel," *DailyCaller.com*, July 11, 2018.

70. "Sen. Lindsey Graham tells Kavanaugh: 'This is the most unethical sham,'" *YouTube.com*, *CBS News*, September 27, 2018.

71. Ken Klukowski, "Democrat Meltdown on Kavanaugh: 'Complicit in Evil,' 'Path to Tyranny,'" *Breitbart.com*, July 31, 2018.

72. Brad Slager, "How the Christine Ford Testimony Exposed the Democrat Smear Machine," *RedState.com*, September 28, 2018.

73. Jennifer Harper, "Broadcasters grant only 4% of Brett Kavanaugh news coverage to judge's side of story: Study," *WashingtonTimes.com*, September 26, 2018.

74. Mark Levin, "Analyzing the media coverage of Judge Brett Kavanaugh," *Life, Liberty & Levin, Youtube.com*, October 7, 2018.

75. John Nolte, "Nolte: *NBC News* Hid Information that Would Have Cleared Kavanaugh of Avenatti Rape Allegations," *Breitbart.com*, October 26, 2018.

76. "Sen. Lindsey Graham tells Kavanaugh: 'This is the most unethical sham,'" *CBS News*, The Kavanaugh Hearings, *YouTube.com*, September 27, 2018.

77. Ibid.

78. Ellen Cranley and Michelle Mark, "Here are all the sexual-misconduct allegations against Brett Kavanaugh, *BusinessInsider.com*, September 27, 2018.

79. Beth Baumann, "Allie Beth Stuckey: I Feel Physically Ill Over What Dems Are Doing to Kavanaugh (VIDEO)," *Townhall.com*, September 28, 2018.

80. Brian Naylor, "Brett Kavanaugh Offers Fiery Defense In Hearing That Was A National Cultural Moment," *NPR.org*, September 28, 2018.

81. Janice Shaw Crouse, "Kavanaugh's Watershed SCOTUS Testimony," *AmericanThinker.com*, September 29, 2018.

82. Christopher Caldwell, Kavanaugh Conservatives vs. Booker Democrats, *WeeklyStandard.com*, October 5, 2018.

83. Kyle Smith, Brett Kavanaugh's History-Changing Speech, *NationalReview.com*, September 28, 2018.

84. John Haltiwanger, "Kavanaugh delivers fiery, emotional opening remarks in Senate hearing, claims his life has been 'totally and permanently destroyed,'" *BusinessInsider.com*, September 27, 2018.

85. Emily Goodin, David Martosko, and Francesca Chambers, "A mother's pride: Supreme Court nominee Brett Kavanaugh's mom tears up after he pays tribute to his family during his opening statement, amid chaotic protests earlier in the day," *Daily-Mail.co.uk*, September 4, 2018; updated September 5, 2018.

86. Matt Vespa, "Trump On Christine Blasey Ford: 'I Had To Even The Playing Field' In Kavanaugh Confirmation Battle,'" *Townhall-.com*, October 8, 2018.

87. Jessica Cantrera and Ian Shapira, "Christine Blasey Ford's family has been nearly silent amid outpouring of support," *WashingtonPost.com*, September 27, 2018.

88. Caroline Hallemann, "Read the Full Transcript of Christine Blasey Ford's Opening Statement at Brett Kavanaugh's Hearing," *TownAndCountryMag.com*, September 27, 2018.

89. John Nolte, "Prosecutor's senate report outlines 9 reasons why Christine Blasey Ford not credible," *Breitbart.com*, October 1, 2018.

90. Ben Sellers, "Mitchell Report Reveals Many Holes in Ford's So-Called Credible Testimony," *LibertyHeadlines.com*, October 1, 2018.

91. Phillip Klein, "Rachel Mitchell's memo is damaging to Christine Blasey Ford's case against Brett Kavanaugh," *WashingtonExaminer.com*, October 1, 2018.

92. Brad Slager, How the Christine Ford Testimony Exposed the Democrat Smear Machine, *RedState.com*, September 28, 2018.

93. Chris Enloe, "Christine Ford's attorney's reveal significant development concerning her Kavanaugh allegations," *TheBlaze.com*, October 7, 2018.

94. Jack Crowe, "Christine Blasey Ford wants to move on," *NationalReview.com*, October 7, 2018.

95. The Horn editorial team, "Kavanaugh accuser drops all her allegations," *TheHornNews.com*, October 8, 2018.

96. Margot Cleveland, "Christine Blasey Ford's changing Kavanaugh assault story leaves her short on credibility," *USAtoday.com*, October 3, 2018.

97. Katie Reilly, "Read Hillary Clinton's 'Basket of Deplorables' Remarks About Donald Trump Supporters," *Time.com*, September 10, 2016.

98. GOPUSA Staff, "The Mysterious Case of Tawana Brawley' goes in-depth on the lie that made Al Sharpton famous," *GOPUSA.com*, November 27, 2018.

99. Al Sharpton, *imdb.com*.

100. *Politics Nation With Al Sharpton, MSNBC.com/politicsnation*

101. Jean Kaufman, "Revisiting Tawana Brawley and Al Sharpton," *PJmedia.com*, December 30, 2014.

102. Joel Shannon, "1,600 men say they believe Christine Blasey Ford in full-page newspaper ad," *USAtoday.com*, September 26, 2018.

103. Daily Mail reporter, "PICTURED: Tawana Brawley still hiding in Virginia 25 years after historic gang rape case that turned out to be a hoax," *DailyMail.co.uk*, December 23, 2012.

104. Washington Free Beacon staff, "Sharpton Can't Admit Tawana Brawley Hoax," *FreeBeacon.com*, October 8, 2013.

105. Jean Kaufman, "Revisiting Tawana Brawley and Al Sharpton," Page 2, *PJmedia*.com, December 30, 2014.

106. Ibid, Page 1.

107. Jim Meyers, "16 Facts About Al Sharpton The Media Won't Tell You," *NewsMax.com*, December 9, 2014.

108. Katie Reilly, "Read Hillary Clinton's 'Basket of Deplorables' Remarks About Donald Trump Supporters," *Time.com*, September 10, 2016.

109. Snejana Farberov, "Home is where the POTUS is: Al Sharpton returns to White House 'for his 73RD visit' with Obama to discuss problems facing minorities," *DailyMail.co.uk*, February 27, 2015; updated February 28, 2018.

110. Katie Reilly, "Read Hillary Clinton's 'Basket of Deplorables' Remarks About Donald Trump Supporters," *Time.com*, September 10, 2016.

111. National Center for Educational Statistics, *nces.ed.gov*.

112. "How many professors are there in the United States?" *Quora.com*.

113. Mitchell Langbert, Anthony J. Quain, and Daniel B. Klein, "Faculty Voter Registration in Economics, History, Journalism, Law, and Psychology," Econ Journal Watch, *econjwatch.org*, September, 2016.

114. Jenna Lawrence, "AEI Panel: Marxists outnumber conservatives in social sciences," *CampusReform.org*, June 13, 2016.

115. Mark Moran, "False Memories: As Believable as the Real Thing?" *WebMD.com*, December 4, 2000.

116. "What Are False Memories," False Memory Syndrome Foundation, *fmsonline.org*.

Chapter Two References

1. Matt Vespa, "Let's Be Honest: The Kavanaugh Allegations Are Nothing More Than A Political Hit Job," *Townhall.com*, September 24, 2018.

2. Erin Schaff for *The New York Times*, "Brett Kavanaugh's Opening Statement: Full Transcript," *NYtimes.com*, September 26, 2018; Updated September 27, 2018.

3. Ibid.

4. Ibid.

5. Brad Slager, "How the Christine Ford Testimony Exposed the Democrat Smear Machine," *RedState.com*, September 28, 2018

6. David French, "The Character Assassination of Brett Kavanaugh," *NationalReview.com*, September 7, 2018.

7. Kurt Schlichter, "Remember That Our Opponents Are Insane Crazy People," *Townhall.com*, October 11, 2018.

8. NewsMax Wires, "Kavanaugh Faces '11th Hour Character Assassination,'" *NewsMax.com*, September 13, 2018.

9. Carrie Severino, *Confirm-Kavanaugh.com*, September, 2018.

10. Matt Vespa, "TRIGGERED: Lesson From Democrats' Kavanaugh Confirmation Nonsense: Belief Is Not Evidence," *Townhall.com*, October 9, 2018.

11. Beth Baumann, "Kellyanne Conway: Many Women, Myself Included, Saw Their Husbands, Sons, Brothers in Kavanaugh," *Townhall.com*, October 7, 2018.

12. Sean Hannity, "Sean Hannity: The left's Kavanaugh tactics should disgust every American," *FoxNews.com*, September 25, 2018.

13. Beth Baumann, "Allie Beth Stuckey: I Feel Physically Ill Over What Dems Are Doing to Kavanaugh (VIDEO)," *Townhall.com*, September 30, 2018.

14. Beth Baumann, "ICYMI: Stephen Colbert Writer Admits She's 'Glad We Ruined Brett Kavanaugh's Life,'" *Townhall.com*, October 9, 2018.

15. *The Ingraham Angle*, "Gingrich: Dems Displayed 'Most Despicable Behavior by a Major Party in Modern History,'" *FoxNews.com*, September 27, 2018 (Video on *YouTube.com.*)

16. Cortney O'Brien, "Trump: I Told Kavanaugh This Was Going to Be a 'Piece of Cake,'" *Townhall.com*, October 8, 2018.

17. Gregg Re, "President Trump apologizes to Brett Kavanaugh and his family at ceremonial swearing-in as Supreme Court Justice," *FoxNews.com*, October 8, 2018.

18. Ken Klukowski, "Democrat Meltdown on Kavanaugh: 'Complicit in Evil,' 'Path to Tyranny,'" *Breitbart.com*, July 31, 2018.

19. Jacqueline Thomsen, "Booker: Those who don't oppose Kavanaugh are 'complicit in the evil,'" *TheHill.com*, July 24, 2018.

20. Charlie Nash, "Google Design Lead David Hogue: 'Evil' Republicans Will 'Descend into Flames' of Hell," *Breitbart.com*, October 8, 2018.

21. Walter E. Williams, "It's Our Constitution – Not Kavanaugh," *Townhall.com*, September 12, 2018.

22. Jason Devaney, "Kavanaugh Goes on Defense: 'I Am a Pro-Law Judge," *NewsMax.com*, October 4, 2018.

23. For RSS, "Brett Kavanaugh defends his emotional testimony in WSJ op-ed – here's what he said," *TheBlaze.com*, October 4, 2018.

24. Myron Magnet, From the Magazine, "James Madison and the Dilemmas of Democracy: What kind of government did the Father of the Constitution envision?" *City-Journal.org*, Winter, 2011.

25. Bill Federer, "How Tyrants Arise: Plato's Eerily Accurate Words," *WND.com*, October 10, 2015.

26. Mark Grannis, "Liberty Quotation: Lord Acton on the Tyranny of the Majority," *LPMaryland.org*, Posted June 25, 2014; Updated June 25, 2014.

27. Marvin Simkin, "Individual Rights," *Los Angeles Times*, January 12, 1992. (Article available at *Articles.LATimes.com*.)

28. David Horowitz on "Glenn Beck," *Fox News* Network, September 4, 2009; "Reformed Radical on Militant Movement," Transcript of September 4, 2009 program, *FoxNews.com*, published September 8, 2009, last update January 14, 2015.

29. David Horowitz, "Betty Friedan's Secret Communist Past," Salon, *Writing.Upenn.edu*, January 18, 1999.

30. *GPO.gov*; "Supreme Court Decisions Overruled by Subsequent Decision."

31. Leah Barkoukis, "Schumer: 'There's No Presumption Of Innocence' for Kavanaugh," *Townhall.com*, September 26, 2018.

32. Cortney O'Brien, "Booker: I Don't Care If Kavanaugh Is Innocent Or Guilty. Let's Move On," *Townhall.com*, October 3, 2018.

33. Frank Holmes, "Hypocrites: Dems Elect 4 Men Accused of Sexual Misconduct," *TheHornNews.com*, November 10, 2018.

34. "DNC Co-Chair Denies Accusations of Domestic Violence," *TheHornNews.com*, August 13, 2018. (*The Associated Press* contributed to this article.)

35. Los Angeles County Democratic Party, Endorsements: November 6, 2018 Midterm General Election, *LACDP.org/Endorsements*.

36. Adam Edelman, "Former Aide Accuses Rep. Bobby Scott of Sexual Misconduct," *NBCNews.com*, December 15, 2017; Updated December 18, 2017.

37. John Sexton, "Progressives: White Women Need Accountability And 'A Lot Of Learning' After Failing To Vote Uniformly For Left-Wing Candidates," *HotAir.com*, November 7, 2018.

38. Ibid.

39. Lauretta Brown, "Patricia Heaton, Conservative Women Respond to the Women's March Shaming White Women for Voting Republican," *Townhall.com*, November 8, 2018.

40. Allie Stuckey, "White Women Don't Need Your Saving," *Townhall.com*, November 8, 2018.

41. The Horn editorial team, "Top CNN star caught in nasty Trump lie," *TheHornNews.com*, October 15, 2018.

42. Rich Noyes, "CNN Gives Virtually No Air Time to Pro-Kavanaugh Evidence," *NewsBusters.com*, September 19, 2018.

43. John Nolte, "Nolte: *NBC News* Hid Information That Would Have Cleared Kavanaugh Of Avenatti Rape Allegations," *Breitbart.com*, October 26, 2018.

44. John Sexton, "NBC's Kate Snow: Here's Why We Didn't Publish That Story On Avenatti's 2nd Witness Until Now," *HotAir.com*, October 27, 2018.

45. Bill D'Agostino and Nicholas Fondacaro, "What Memo? NBC Ignores Prosecutor Memo Questioning Ford's Claims," *NewsBusters.com*, October 1, 2018.

46. Michael Kunzelman, Michael Biesecker & Martha Mendoza, *The Associated Press*, "Third Kavanaugh accuser has extensive legal history," *WashingtonTimes.com*, Sunday, September 30, 2018.

47. Kate Snow, "Kavanaugh accuser Julie Swetnick speaks out on sexual abuse allegations," *NBCnews.com*, October 1, 2018.

48. John Nolte, "Nolte: 28 Reasons Julie Swetnick's Kavanaugh Allegations Are Total Garbage," *Breitbart.com*, October 3, 2018.

49. Matt Vespa, "Tapping Out: Christine Blasey Ford Won't Pursue Her Sexual Misconduct Allegations Against Justice Kavanaugh," *Townhall.com*, October 7, 2018.

50. As seen on Hannity, "Sen. Graham Blasts NBC for Julie Swetnick Interview, Coverage of Kavanaugh Allegations," *Insider.FoxNews.com*, October 1, 2018. (Video & Text)

51. Mike Brest, "Sen. Graham: NBC Has Been A 'Co-Conspirator' In The Destruction Of Kavanaugh," *DailyCaller.com*, October 1, 2018.

52. Bill D'Agostino, "TV News Buries Trump's Defeat of ISIS in Iraq and Syria," *NewsBusters.com*, October 23, 2018.

53. Joseph Curl, "How much does CNN hate Trump? 93% of coverage is negative," *WashingtonTimes.com*, May 23, 2017.

54. Melanie Arter, "NYT Defends Publishing Short Story Imagining Assassination of Trump," *CNSNews.com*, October 26, 2018.

55. Brian McNicoll, "AP Falsely Reports Trump is Kicking Immigrants Out Of The Military," *Accuracy In Media, AIM.org*, July 9, 2018.

56. Frank Holmes, "5 Biggest Media LIES about Trump...This Month!" *TheHornNews.com*, December 26, 2017.

57. Kaylee McGhee, "96 Percent of Google Search Results on Trump Slant Left," *LibertyHeadlines.com*, August 28, 2018.

58. Rich Noyes, "Study: Economic Boom Largely Ignored as TV's Trump Coverage Hits 92% Negative," *NewsBusters.com*, October 9, 2018.

59. Jennifer Harper, "Broadcasters grant only 4% of Brett Kavanaugh news coverage to judge's side of story: Study," *WashingtonTimes.com*, September 26, 2018.

60. John Nolte, "Nolte: *NBC News* Hid Information that Would Have Cleared Kavanaugh of Avenatti Rape Allegations," *Breitbart.com*, October 26, 2018.

61. Mark Levin, *Life, Liberty & Levin,* October 7, 2018. *Youtube.com* video titled: *Life, Liberty & Levin* 10/7/18| Breaking *Fox News* October 7, 2018.

62. Brian Montololi, "Study finds harsh media coverage for Obama," *CBSnews.com*, October 17, 2011.

63. Matt Vespa, "Let's Be Honest: The Kavanaugh Allegations Are Nothing More Than A Political Hit Job," *Townhall.com*, September 24, 2018.

64. Benny Johnson, "Flashback: Clarence Thomas Calls Sexual Misconduct Allegations Against Him A 'High-Tech Lynching,'" *DailyCaller.com*, September 17, 2918.

65. Ian C. Friedman, "A High-Tech Lynching For Uppity Blacks," *IANCFriedman.com*, November 3, 2011.

66. Paul Sperry, "'Nothing to Gain,' Kavanaugh Accuser Raises Nearly $1 Million," *RealClearInvestigations.com*, October 29, 2018.

67. Danielle Garrand, "Ford speaks out in rare statement since Kavanaugh hearings," *MSN.com*, November 27, 2018.

68. Paul Sperry, "'Nothing to Gain,' Kavanaugh Accuser Raises Nearly $1 Million," *RealClearInvestigations.com*, October 29, 2018.

69. Ibid.

70. Luppe B. Luppen and Hunter Walker, "Justice Kavanaugh declines more than $600,000 raised in GoFundMe campaign," *Yahoo News, Sports.Yahoo.com*, October 30, 2018.

71. Paul Sperry, "'Nothing to Gain,' Kavanaugh Accuser Raises Nearly $1 Million," *RealClearInvestigations.com*, October 29, 2018.

72. Aris Folley, "Women across the world send postcards to Christine Blasey Ford to show support," *TheHill.com*, October 11, 2018.

73. Nicholas Hautman, "Ellen DeGeneres, Mariska Hargitay and More Stars Support Christine Blasey Ford During Brett Kavanaugh Hearing," *USmagzine.com*, September 27, 2018.

74. Ibid.

75. "1,600 men voice support for Christine Blasey Ford in *New York Times* ad," *TheGuardian.com*, September 26, 2018.

76. Kelly McLaughlin, "Hundreds of women who have graduated from Yale have signed a letter in support of a classmate who accused Brett Kavanaugh of exposing himself to her," *ThisIsInsider.com*, September 24, 2018.

77. Holton Alumnae in Support of Dr. Christine Blasey Ford, "We Stand With Dr. Christine Blasey Ford." *StandWithBlaseyFord-.com*.

78. Katie Pavlich, "Christine Blasey Ford Makes a Shameful Public Appearance...on Behalf of *Sports Illustrated*," *Townhall.com*, December 12, 2018.

79. R.J. Rummel, "Death by Government: Stalin Beat Hitler but Mao Surpassed Both," *OrthodoxyToday.org*, December 4, 2015.

80. Life Site News Staff, "China commits 'staggering' 23 million abortions per year, according to US State Dept.," *LifeSite-News.com*, April 15, 2016.

81. Matt Schiavenza, "Today's China Statistic: Abortions," *TheAtlantic.com*, March 19, 2013.

82. Thomas Sowell, *Inside American Education: The Decline, The Deception, The Dogmas*, The Free Press, 1993.

83. David Horowitz, at Duke University in Duran, NC, discussing his book, *The Professors: The 101 Most Dangerous Academics in America*.

84. David Horowitz, *One Party Classroom: How Radical Professors at America's Top Colleges Indoctrinate Students and Undermine Our Democracy*, Crown Forum, 2009.

85. Janice Fiamengo, "To Understand Christine Blasey Ford, Take a Look at Palo Alto University," *YouTube.com*, October 6, 2018.

86. Ibid.

87. David Horowitz, "Betty Friedan's Secret Communist Past," Salon, *Writing.Upenn.edu*, January 18, 1999.

88. Tammy Bruce, *The New Thought Police: Inside The Left's Assault On Free Speech And Free Minds,* Forum, 2001.

89. Kevin Mooney, "New Film Exposes Apparent Lack of Academic Freedom in U.S.,"*CNSNews.com*, October 8, 2007.

90. David Horowitz, *Indoctrination U: The Left's War Against Academic Freedom*, Encounter Books, 2009. *EncounterBooks.com*.

91. Ibid.

92. Jarrett Stepman, "Made-Up Hate Crimes Out of Control as Victimhood Is Extolled on College Campuses," *WesternJournal-.com*, October 19, 2018.

93. Caleb Parke, "Hate Crimes And Hoaxes: 10 Campus Stories Debunked In 2017," *FoxNews.com*, December 27, 2018.

94. John Sexton, "Another fake hate crime uncovered by police," *HotAir.com*, April 10, 2018.

95. Ibid.

96. John Sexton, "A Fake, Anti-Muslim Hate Crime In Canada," *HotAir.com*, January 15, 2018.

97. Brianna Heldt, "Parents Sue After Son Is Falsely Accused of Sexual Assault by 'Mean Girls' at High School," *Townhall.com*, October 10, 2018.

98. *The Associated Press*, "Lawsuit accuses 'mean girls' at Pa. school of targeting boy with false sexual assault accusations," *PennLive.com*, October 5, 2018.

99. Paul Peirce, "Seneca Valley defends its actions in 'Mean Girls' case," *APnews.com*, October 13, 2018.

100. Brianna Heldt, "Parents Sue After Son Is Falsely Accused of Sexual Assault by 'Mean Girls' at High School," *Townhall.com*, October 10, 2018.

101. College Fix Staff, "Georgetown professor calls for white male Republican senators to suffer 'miserable deaths,'" *The-CollegeFix.com*, October 1, 2018.

102. Stephen Montemayor, "Rosemount educator on leave after tweeting 'kill Kavanaugh?'" *StarTribune.com*, October 9, 2018.

103. Eddie Scarry, "Media convict Brett Kavanaugh and GOP on grounds of being white males," *WashingtonExaminer.com*, September 22, 2018.

104. John Sexton, "Reporter Andy Ngo: The List Of Fake Hate Crimes Is Pretty Long (Update), *HotAir.com*, February 18, 2019

105. Ann Coulter, "White Supremacists Ate My Homework," *Breitbart.com*, January 16, 2019.

106. Phelim McAleer, "Flashback: Woman Lies About Being Raped to the Senate Judiciary Committee," *Townhall.com*, October 2, 2018.

107. Katie Pavlich, "Kavanaugh Accuser Admits: I Made Up Claims of Sexual Assault to 'Get Attention,'" *Townhall.com*, November 2, 1018.

108. Because I Am A Boy, "Boys are guilty even when innocent," *Youtube.com*, January 30, 2013.

109. Joe Roberts, "Woman jailed for falsely accusing teenager of raping her in public toilets," *Metro.co.uk*, October 12, 2018.

110. Mary Katharine Ham, "Fantastic Lies: 10 Appalling Moments From the Duke Lacrosse Case." *TheFederalist.com*, March 16, 2016.

111. Jazz Shaw, "False Rape Accuser Heading To Prison," *HotAir-.com*, June 8, 2018.

112. *AP News*, "Woman who made false rape claim gets 1 year in jail," *APnews.com*, August 23, 2018.

113. Marvin Clemons, "Rape charges against 4 California dentists dismissed after video contradicts woman's story," *News3lv.com*, October 1, 2018.

114. Matt Vespa, "Believe All Women Crashes Into Wall: Woman Forced To Apologize After She Falsely Accused Nine-Year-Old Of Sexual Assault," *Townhall.com*, October 15, 2018.

115. Rowan Scarborough, "False reports of sexual assault not as rare as claimed, studies show," *WashingtonTimes.com*, Sunday, October 7, 2018.

116. Associate Editor, "#HimToo Gains Attention After Uncorroborated Kavanaugh Allegations," *LibertyHeadlines.com*, October 14, 2018.

117. Michael Barnes, "Police Body Camera Footage Exposes Motorist's 'Lynching' Lie;" "FALSE ACCUSATION: 'I was just bullied by a racist cop, who threatened to pull me out of the car...'" *LibertyHeadlines.com*, May 11, 2018.

118. Lindsay Kimble, "Can a Married Man Have Dinner with Another Woman? Mike Pence Doesn't Think So – and the Internet Has Lots of Feelings," *People.com*, March 31, 2017.

119. Olga Khazan, "How Pence's Dudely Dinners Hurt Women, *TheAtlantic.com*, March 30, 2017

120. Aaron Blake, "Mike Pence doesn't dine alone with other women. And we're all shocked," *WashingtonPost.com*, March 30, 2017.

121. Thomas D. Williams, "Witches United to Cast 'Binding Spell' On Trump and Followers," *Breitbart.com*, February 24, 2017.

122. Lifestyle, "Witches plan to cast spell on Donald Trump and his supporters Friday night," *TheBlaze.com*, February 24, 2017.

123. As seen on *Fox & Friends Weekend*, "Witches Cast Mass Spell with Hopes of Removing Trump from Office," *Insider.Fox-News.com*, February 25, 2017.

124. Aaron Klein, "Exclusive – Juanita Broaddrick Provides Never Before Published Details On Bill Clinton's Rape," *Breitbart.com*, July 10, 2016.

125. Valerie Richardson, "Broaddrick: Sen. Feinstein had no interest in my rape allegation against Bill Clinton," *Washington-Times.com*, September 19, 2018.

126. Timothy Meads, "Brooklyn Witches Host 'Ritual to Hex Brett Kavanaugh'" *Townhall.com*, October 10, 2018.

127. *National Right to Life News Today*, "National Right to Life Commends President Trump For His Selection of Judge Brett Kavanaugh as Successor to Justice Kennedy," *NationalRightTo-LifeNews.org*, July 10, 2018.

128. Aris Folley, "Exorcist to hold mass for Kavanaugh to counteract witches 'hexing' him," *TheHill.com*, October 18, 2018.

129. Joshua Paladino, "215 Illegal Aliens in NC Charged with More than 700 Child Sex Crimes," *LibertyHeadlines.com*, January 8, 2019.

130. "President Donald J. Trump's Address to the Nation on the Crisis at the Border," *WhiteHouse.gov*, January 8, 2019.

131. *Rainn,* The Criminal Justice System: Statistics. The majority of Sexual Assaults Are Not Reported to the Police. *Rainn.org*.

132. Tony Gonzalez, *The Tennessean*, "Study: Sexual Assaults Greatly Underreported," *USAtoday.com*, November 19, 2013.

133. Joshua Paladino, "215 Illegal Aliens in NC Charged with More than 700 Child Sex Crimes," *LibertyHeadlines.com*, January 8, 2019.

134. Michael Barnes, "Alabama Rep. Rips Media for Ignoring Victim Families of Criminal Aliens," *LibertyHeadlines.com*, January 16, 2019.

135. Jens Manuel Krogstad, Jeffery S. Passel and D'Vera Cohn, "5 facts about illegal immigration in the U.S.," *PewResearch.org*, November 28, 2018.

136. Paul Bedard, "DHS: 23% of all federal prisoners are illegals, just 7 of 42,034 saved from deportation," *WashingtonExaminer-.com*, August 9, 2018.

137. Wayne Allyn Root, "I Want a Wall Just Like Israel's," *Townhall.com*, January 13, 2018.

138. Hans A. von Spakovsky and Grant Strobl, "What the Media Won't Tell You About Illegal Immigration and Criminal Activity," *Heritage.org*, March 13, 2017.

139. Wayne Allyn Root, "Harry Reid Exposes Greatest Liberal Scam Of All-Time," *Townhall.com*, January 20, 2019.

140. Frank Holmes, "Ugly: The 10 things Democrats hate (that Americans love), *TheHornNews.com*, February 9, 2019.

About The Author

Michael T. Petro, Jr. is a veteran of the U.S. Navy. Initially he worked in naval security, and later served in the gunnery division aboard the USS Kennebec during the Vietnam War. After returning to his native state of Ohio, he earned a Bachelor of Arts Degree (Magna Cum Laude) from Cleveland State University.

When relocating to California he earned a Master of Science Degree in Psychology and a Master of Arts Degree in Education from California State University at Los Angeles. Michael initially worked as an aide and counselor in psychiatric hospitals in the greater Los Angeles area. Later he worked extensively as a researcher, training coordinator, and manager at an alcohol and drug recovery program located on Skid Row in Los Angeles.

Before leaving California, Michael received a National Leadership Award from the National Headquarters of the Volunteers of America. The award was presented for his success in restoring operational integrity to a dysfunctional alcohol and drug recovery program and for his efforts to create drug-free zones within the Skid Row community.

Today, Michael works as a writer, editor, and publisher in Cleveland, Ohio, helping aspiring writers become published authors. For more information visit *PetroPublications.com*.

Fact Sheet Number One

The Evidence

This page contains all the evidence that the FBI, American Bar Association, Senate Judiciary Committee, Democrat Senate Judiciary Committee Smear Machine, Democrat Media Smear Machine, and the Clinton Smear Machine produced to prove beyond a reasonable doubt that Justice Brett Kavanaugh is guilty of personal or professional misconduct as an adolescent or as an adult.

Fact Sheet Number Two

Corroborating Witnesses

This page contains the names of all the people who have come forward to serve as credible corroborating witnesses for those who have accused Justice Brett Kavanaugh of personal or professional misconduct as an adolescent or as an adult.